P9-CDG-880

The Complete Book of Curtains, Drapes & Blinds

LIVINGSTON PUBLIC LIBRARY
10 Robert H. Harp Drive
Livingston, NJ 07039

747.3
BAK

9-24-09
h9

THE COMPLETE BOOK OF CURTAINS, DRAPES,
AND BLINDS. Copyright © 2009 by Anova Books. All
rights reserved. Printed in Singapore.

For information, address St. Martin's Press,
175 Fifth Avenue, New York, N.Y. 10010.

www.stmartins.com

The written instructions, photographs, designs, patterns,
and projects in this volume are intended for personal
use of the reader and may be reproduced for that
purpose only.

Library of Congress Cataloging-in-Publication Data
Available Upon Request

ISBN-13: 978-0-312-58653-9
ISBN-10: 0-312-58653-1

First St. Martin's Griffin Edition: September 2009

10 9 8 7 6 5 4 3 2 1

The Complete Book of Curtains, Drapes & Blinds

Design ideas for every type of window treatment

Wendy Baker

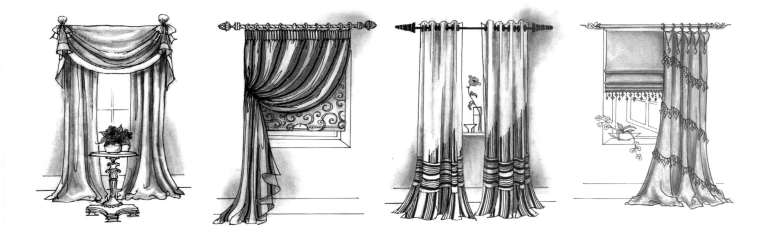

St. Martin's Griffin
New York

Contents

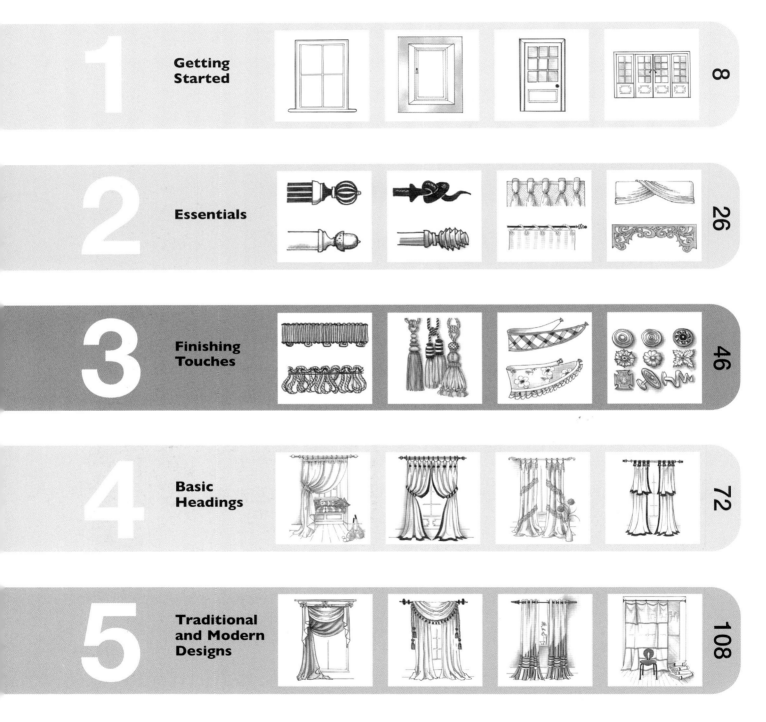

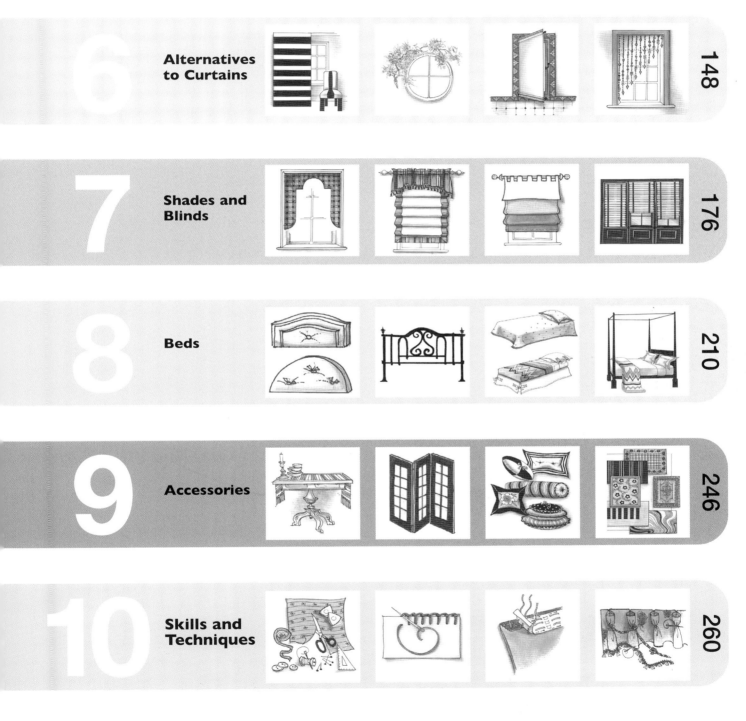

How to use this book...

This is a giant book of ideas for window coverings. I know for sure that it will solve all your window problems and maybe a few others along the way! If you know my Sketchbooks—and most decorators have at least one of them in their library—then you will know that my books are just filled with ideas for window coverings. These are always in the form of black line sketches—this way you can see the design clearly—and there are very few words. My books are not really for reading, they are there to lead you through the complicated business of selecting the right drapes or shade for a particular style of window.

The problem these days is that there is so much to choose from. Never have there been so many poles and finials on the market, never have the fabrics been so colorful and the prints so inspiring, the textures so touchable. It must seem daunting to be faced with so many choices when all you want is a simple pair of drapes—and this is where my book comes in. Everything that you need to know about selecting the best fabric, the correct pole and the right style for almost any window type is clearly shown in these pages. If you want to see what the design will look like in your color scheme, then color it yourself just like a painting book.

Chapter One is all about getting started. Here you will find information on making an initial plan of action, creating the perfect color scheme and choosing the right general style of drapery or shade for many different window situations. This section also has information about the different types of fabric that will be suitable for window coverings, and suggests how each could best be used.

Chapter Two covers all the essential information that will help you make your initial choices. In this chapter you will find everything you need to know about the different drapery systems currently on the market. It also looks at some of the finial designs available for drapery poles, and the basic variations for drape and valance headings, and for pelmets.

In Chapter 3 we are looking at those little finishing touches that will make your drapes extra special—trims, ropes, tassels, tie-backs and hold-backs. Most of the basic types are illustrated here, although each will come in an endless selection of colorways and with some minor variations. At the end of this chapter you will find a selection of full drapery illustrations, which will give you some great ideas as to how the trims and other finishing touches can be used to make your drapes unique.

In the next chapter we move on to headings. The heading you use will set the style of your drapes, so it is vital that you spend some time here to choose exactly the right design for your room. All the different heading types are featured actually on drapes, valance or pelmet, with the correct drapery system in place, so you can really get an idea of the full effect you might be able to achieve.

Chapter 5 covers a range of drapery designs. Here we look at both traditional and modern styles, using swags and tails, how to treat bay windows, Italian stringing, dress curtains, and some options for voiles. The captions highlight the main elements that are creating the look, so you will find it easy to understand how to get the same kind of effect yourself.

Of course some windows are just not suitable for drapes, so in Chapter 6 we look at some other options for window treatments. In this chapter you will find information and illustrations covering panels, café curtains, portières, difficult windows and other window dressing ideas.

If you are more interested in shades and blinds, go to Chapter 7. Again there are clear illustrations of all the basic shade types: Roman; Austrian; Linen fold; Cascade; Oriental; and London. In addition, this chapter also covers lambrequins and shutters, including wooden Venetian shades and shades for Velux® windows.

In the bedroom the drapes are often coordinated with the bed, so in Chapter 8 you will find some design ideas for many different bed styles, as well as a host of options for children's rooms.

Choosing exactly the right accessories can make all the difference to an interior design scheme. In Chapter 9 we look at some of the main accessories you could use, such as table covers, screens, pillows, throws, rugs and even flowers.

Finally, in Chapter 10, you will find the basic skills and techniques needed to create most of the drapes and shades shown in this book. There are entire books on drapery and shade making so this skills section cannot be completely comprehensive, but it will certainly allow you to make most of the designs yourself.

When you have chosen a couple of designs you think might work in your room, try coloring them up in the colors of the fabrics you will be using to see the full effect. You don't have to be an artist to do this, so don't be afraid! You can also try mixing and matching elements—although with the choice available in these pages I would be surprised if there wasn't something exactly right...

1

Getting Started

Design plan…

Whether you are an interior decorator or a homeowner, the best advice anyone can give you before you tackle a new design project is: take your time; make a list of the basic essentials. Ask yourself a few questions… Do you have a clean slate or must you work around furniture that you already have, even if you don't really like it? Is your choice of fabric dependent on the color of your carpets? Do you have enough money to do the job properly, or will you have to make compromises? This may lead to some hard decisions, but it is essential to consider all these things at the start—if you begin without a plan you can go around in circles and that will work out expensive in the long run.

First, decide what sort of feel you want to achieve in the room—spacious and minimal with a loft feel, perhaps, or country cozy with a homemade look. Then look at what you are working with and how you could achieve the feel you want. For instance, perhaps the room is north-facing with cold light, or the ceilings are tall so it seems unfriendly. You can change the feel in the north-facing room by choosing a warm-toned fabric, perhaps with a texture, and emphasize those tall ceilings by selecting a fabric in a cool color, such as aqua or lime green, to give a feeling of airiness and space.

The first consideration in any interior design scheme is generally the flooring. If you need to keep the existing flooring find a spare piece if possible, so you can include it in your color board. If you can start from scratch, have plain wood floors or a neutral carpet and cover with simple rugs, which can easily be changed when you want a different look. Rugs these days are wonderful and not that expensive.

The next priority is your furniture and how it will fit in with your new design. Sometimes existing furniture doesn't work with a different color scheme and it can be costly to buy new. There are ways to minimize the effect of existing items of course—you could use throws to cover them up, or have them reupholstered. However, sometimes a clean sweep is the best option… and you can always photograph unwanted pieces and sell them on eBay! If you are keeping furniture and the upholstery is nearly new, again find a similar sample, or something similar, for your color board.

Finally, look at the walls. In general, changing the wall color will be the basis of your new scheme, but if you have a very special wallcovering that you need to retain you will need to include a sample—or something similar—on your color board.

The right color scheme...

My advice to anyone when choosing a color scheme is to play down the color palette to begin with—you can always add stronger colors as the scheme progresses. It might be fun at first to have a lime green wall and purple rugs scattered around, but six months later you will probably wish you had been a tiny bit more reserved in your color choices! It really is best to go for more muted tones. I don't mean beige, beige and more beige; perhaps try gray for a change—most colors work well with it. I created a lovely scheme with smoky blue for drapes and bed covers, walls two tones lighter and paintwork in a soft stone color. Add a rug in the same colors plus a muted pink thread running through the design, and it all looked dreamy.

If you are starting from scratch, choose neutral colors for the basics such as carpets and walls and a deeper tone for drapes and upholstery. Brighter items, such as pillows, can then be added later for emphasis.

Making a color board

The basis for creating any new color scheme is a color board. This doesn't have to be anything fancy, simply a board with samples of all the major items in the room, in the correct colors and approximately the right proportions in relation to each other. If you can't include samples of the actual carpet or wallcovering, something similar in the same color and tone will do. You can usually get small cuttings of fabric from suppliers before buying. When you have made your board, stand back and judge the overall effect. You are looking to achieve a generally muted effect, with perhaps just one or two stronger items to lift the scheme and prevent it being boring. Try to judge the color board in the actual room—different lighting conditions can make quite a difference.

Existing decor

If you are moving into a new house or flat and the walls are newly painted they will probably be white. Developers must buy cheap white paint in huge cans and they seem to slap it on everywhere—but at least this is better than ten years ago when everything was painted magnolia!

If you have a low budget you may decide to save money by "living" with the existing wall color but personally I think this is false economy. It doesn't take very long or cost much to repaint walls, then at least you are starting with the right base color. Perhaps just use a neutral color to start with—don't try to be too clever.

If your upholstery doesn't work with your new wall colors then throw a linen cover or rug over it, until you can afford to change or reupholster it. Otherwise don't tie yourself down with old baggage—move on. No, you can't alter those old drapes to fit your new windows: nothing looks worse than drapes that have been let down or that don't meet in the middle. Manage without drapes for a while until you have the money to do things properly. You can always hang a wonderful colored shawl at the bedroom window temporarily—and you might end up by preferring it like that anyway.

The right style of drapes or shades

It's important to consider the shape, size and function of your window before you decide on the style of drapery or shade to use. Below are a few window styles and some basic guidelines to bear in mind—there are many more sizes and shapes to consider, but if you use this as a rough guide you won't go far wrong.

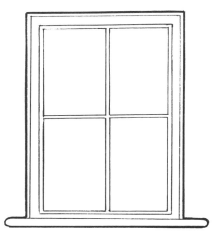

Basic window

▶ A pair of simple drapes on a pole
▶ Short or café-style drapes
▶ A simple shade so as not to overpower the window

Recessed window

▶ Blinds inside the recess should be in translucent fabrics
▶ Pole or pelmet fixed on the outside of the recess—but only if there is enough space either side of the window to stack curtains when in the open position
▶ Short curtains on a swing-arm bracket

Cottage style

▶ Long or short drapes on a pole, but clearing the window frame to let in the maximum light
▶ Shades should be fixed clear of the window frame to allow maximum light

Tips

Never put short drapes on a Georgian window—in fact I don't really like to use short drapes anywhere, unless it is absolutely necessary.
For some ideas on how to treat difficult windows, see Chapter 6.

to suit the window

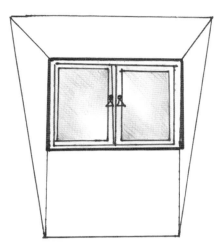

Dormer window

▶ Portière panels
▶ Shades fixed as high as possible
▶ Short drapes on a swing-arm bracket

Georgian window

▶ Long, elegant drapes on a pole or with a pelmet
▶ Valances of any kind
▶ Be creative—everything looks good with Georgian windows

Georgian arched window

▶ If you want to emphasize the shape, see page 166 for ideas
▶ Pole fixed above the arch—make sure it is fixed high enough and the drapes can "stack" out of the way so as not to lose the beautiful shape

Bay windows

▶ A covered lathe (concealed tracking) with long drapes. Can be 2 drapes (one either end), or 3 (one in the middle), or 4 drapes—it depends on the size of the window and the tracking combination
▶ When a bay window is small or you don't want to lose any light, have drapes on a pole across the bay, ignoring its shape completely
▶ Shades and dress drapes
▶ Shades only

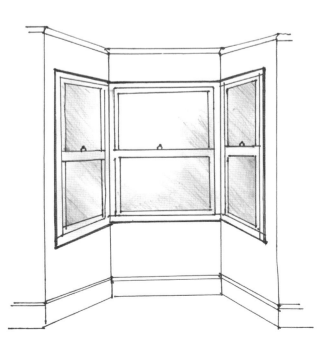

Basic glazed door shapes

Before you consider drapes for doorways, check that the door does not open inwards or the drapery will get in the way whenever you try to open it. You can, of course, have drapes in this situation but the pole or tracking will have to be fixed well above the doorway and when open the drapes must stack back out of the way on either side, so they are completely clear of the opening door.

Half-glazed Georgian-style door

▶ Drapery must be clear when opening door
▶ Avoid fixing a shade to this kind of door. It is rarely successful—if you really have no alternative then maybe a Roman shade might be the best choice
▶ A good solution would be to have sandblasted glass put into the door

Sliding Patio doors

▶ Again, make sure the drapes clear the doorway completely
▶ NEVER have shades on patio doors
▶ In this situation consider having one big drape pulling to one side—but you must have the space at the side of the door to "stack" it

French windows with side windows

► As always, check drapes are clear of the opening of the two central doors—but in this case you can have drapery partly over the side windows, since they do not open

► Be sure that your pole or tracking is heavy enough, especially if your fabric is thick, as this kind of door/window has a wide span

► Your pole will need a center bracket for this width

French windows in a bay

► There are some very nice steel poles that can be shaped to your bay window (see page 33)

► The problem with windows/doors like this is that the bay shape means there is not always enough room to "stack" the drapes at each side—in this case you could stack them partly over the two fixed windows

15

Choosing a design for drapes or shade

Once you have decided on your plan and have a clear picture in your head of what kind of look you want to achieve then you can select your design and fabric. Give yourself a loose budget, as if you start off with no budget in mind you will so often find the costs spiral out of control and inexpensive fabrics are not so easy to track down these days, unless you stick with cottons from India maybe. Next, look at the shape of your window, as not all kinds of drapes or shades work for every window. There is a section in this book to guide you through this. Try to follow these basic rules and it will help you to make the right choice of design for the window as well as for the room.

North-facing windows

If the room faces north, it will generally be fairly dark. Avoid shades that have to be fitted in the window recess, so covering the top part of the window all the time. Definitely don't have a design that needs pelmets or swags and tails, as these will cut out even more of the natural light.

Windows with radiators

Heaters are frequently placed under the windows. This rules out long drapes as you will lose too much heat. You can avoid this by having long dress drapery and then functional shades that will allow the heater to do its job properly.

Tall ceilings and big windows

When the windows are big and tall you have so much more scope—choose a flamboyant print in electric colors or just go for simple translucent neutral-colored shades to let in as much light as possible. The problem with big windows, of course, is that you need a lot of fabric and that means lots of money – but you can cheat and use a simple muslin and add ribbons on the hem. Or put insets of lace and perhaps dye the muslin and the lace.

Low ceilings and big windows

Use a striped fabric to create the illusion of ceiling height. Some windows are not very tall but extremely wide, and then I suggest you use the whole wall—hang the drapes from the ceiling and use the entire wall at the side of the windows to stack the drapery back.

Low ceilings and small windows

Drapes for small windows, generally found in country cottages or in attic rooms, should be kept simple. Fabrics should be plain or small prints in delicate colors—nothing too dark or too bright. I suggest you have a voile curtain with a roller shade behind it to pull down at night. I dislike short drapes but sometimes it is unavoidable—if you have to have them I think they are better just lined but not interlined as then they look short AND chunky!

Open or loft-style rooms

This is a good time to experiment—try using large prints, the bolder the better, or you can play it down by choosing neutral-colored shades and then cover with vast amounts of voile. Put the voile drapes on electric tracking so you can sweep them dramatically right back to take advantage of a spectacular view. My preference is to use panels on electric tracking. There are many designs for panels in this book, and when you have very tall, wide windows, using panels with tracking generally turns out to be a good solution.

Fabric characteristics...

I used to think that the more you paid for a fabric the better it would be, but there are so many fantastic ones on the market, some ridiculously cheap and others that are beyond most people's budgets, I think that your best bet is to go for something that you really like regardless of the cost—and if it's expensive cut down on something else.

If the windows are small steer clear of heavy fabric, as you will block out too much light. Don't choose thin fabric and try to put in blackout lining, as the drapes won't fall properly. All fabrics will fade if exposed to direct sunlight, so in hotter countries or sunny spots consider shutters or voile drapes. However, basically most fabrics can be adapted to suit the designs in this book—and if you are not sure ask your interior decorator or fabric store for advice.

Wools and wool mixes

You have a huge range of woolen fabrics, from the soft pastel shades of fine wool and basic flannels, to chunky tweeds. All make up really well and are best in very simple styles. Simple style curtains made in knobbly tweed look marvellous in a big country house. There are plenty of wool plaids around, if you own a Scottish castle—and softer checks in heather mixtures, which are easy to live with and give a comfortable, warm feel to a barn or farmhouse.

Linen and natural weaves

I love all natural weaves, especially linen, which I like to wear whatever the weather. It looks wonderful when used for drapery or shades—it does generally look crumpled and relaxed, but that is what I like about it. Looks best, as far as I am concerned, when used unlined since it does hang so well. If you have chosen a style of drapes or shades with pin tucks, saddle-stitching or horizontal pleats then this is the fabric to use, as it goes together like a dream.

There are many wonderful colors to choose from. For some time I liked the natural string color, but now I am experimenting and have come up with a lovely soft colored pallete with muted blues, lilac and grays and it looks lovely... so I may get out of my beige rut and be a bit more adventurous!

Tips

Always use thread to match the composition of your drapery fabric.

When buying fabric, check the laundering instructions on the fabric bolt.

Some natural weaves have slubs as part of their composition. These are not faults, but if they are very obvious be aware of where they will fall when measuring and cutting.

Cotton

Most cotton fabrics are relatively inexpensive, which is why they are so popular, I suppose. The only time I use it is for drapes or shades in a kitchen or bathroom since it can be machine washed. Be careful to have a washable lining if the drapes are lined. Children's bedroom drapes are also best in cotton for the same reason. If you use a blackout lining (one of the new soft ones on the market, not the thick smelly rubber kind) and your drapes are machine made, then this is an ideal hardwearing fabric.

Tips

Depending on how cotton is finished it can have a matte or a shiny texture. These special finishes are often removed when the fabric is washed..

Shiny fabrics reflect light, making the room appear bigger. Matte fabrics absorb light, making the room appear smaller.

Check the fabric width—narrow widths will mean you need more lengths of fabric to create your curtains, so what appears to be an inexpensive fabric can end up costing more in the long run.

Velvet

When I think of velvet, I think of cinema seats or formal swags and tails in a theater, but there are some really nice velvets around at present—look for panné velvet and you will find a soft floppy fabric that hangs beautifully when made into drapes. Don't use it for shades. There are lots of cut velvets around and these have a younger feel to them. Another favorite is Paisley printed velvet. Still, if you want formal drapes, then velvet is still the best fabric. It can look special when you overload the drapes with trims, such as bullion fringe mixed with embroidered wide ribbons. You must line velvet, but if it is heavy you can miss out the interlining. Look for chenille, which is nicer than velvet to my mind.

Tips

When using several lengths of fabric with a pile, make sure the pile runs in the same direction on each piece, or they will look as if they are different colors.

Do not cut off selvages when working with velvet, as it frays very badly.

Silks

This is my favorite fabric. As a dress designer in the sixties I used it for everything—it was a great luxury then but now it can be found to suit everyone's pocket. I have used it for palaces and for penthouses and it always looks stunning. There are so many colors to choose from and such wonderful prints around. Also, most fabric manufacturers have embroidered silks now, from India and Japan, which are very popular. When using silk, make sure there is plenty of fullness in the drapes and let the fabric fall on the floor—you can spoil the effect if you skimp on the fabric. Try adding beaded fringing to the leading edge. Depending on the style, I usually line and interline silk drapes unless I am going for a particular casual look—when I use double the amount of fabric. If the type of silk is crumpled and natural then I often leave out the interlining and sometimes even the lining.

Tips

To avoid puckered seams when sewing silk, place a layer of thin tissue paper above and below the seam, then stitch right through it. You can tear the tissue gently away when you have finished..

Silk is very strong, but repeated exposure to direct sunlight will weaken it and eventually cause it to disintegrate. Line silk drapes if you want to use them in a sunny window.

Voiles (sheers)

This delicate translucent fabric is very popular—there are some wonderful embroidered voiles to be found and although some of them are very expensive you will find some from India that are priced more realistically. If you are using voile for shades make sure you have the fabric treated before the shade is made up—most good shade manufacturers will do this. I like to put voile drapes in front of an ordinary roller shade to soften the starkness of the shade and often use Italian stringing to dramatically sweep the drapes to one side on a large window.

Tips

Use lots of fabric when making up voile into drapes, as it looks pathetic when it is too skimpy.

Voile doesn't only have to be used in conjunction with over-drapes—in the right scheme it can look stunning used on its own.

Voiles will not cut out light—use a light-resistant shade behind them.

Dos

These dos are very important, so read this carefully...

1 First of all, spend time deciding on the type of window covering you want.

2 Check that the shade or drapery design is suitable for your window shape.

3 Be careful not to block out too much light, for instance by covering the window with a very heavy pelmet.

4 Check if your window faces north, as this will always be dark and you will need to allow as much light as possible into the room.

5 Choose a fabric that goes with the rest of your soft furnishings, as otherwise you will need to change everything to match your window coverings—could be expensive!

6 Measure your window correctly, especially if you are having shades.

7 When measuring always use a metal retractable tape measure.

8 If you find that the drapes you have chosen still block out too much light, hold them back with a tie-back or hold-back.

9 With certain fabrics you do need to line and interline them to get the best effect, so do spend that extra money on doing this.

10 Do be absolutely sure you are happy with your choice of fabric, especially if it is bright and bold—you will have to live with this for at least 10 years.

Don't skip this list – it is important!

1 Never choose a style of window covering that blocks out too much light; it is depressing to live with, especially in winter.

2 When choosing the fabric try to avoid big bold prints in small rooms.

3 If your windows are tall don't even think about short drapery, whatever the reason, as they will look ridiculous. If there is no other way around it— don't have curtains at all!

4 Don't make the mistake of having drapes over a window that opens inwards—the treatment has to clear the opening window.

5 If you are having a valance or pelmet with the drapes don't make them too shallow, as this is a common mistake. Be sure you look at the window and the length of the drapes before making the final choice—be bold with your decision.

6 If you try to put light-resistant lining in a flimsy fabric you will have a disaster on your hands, so avoid this at all costs. Use a roller shade behind the drapes instead.

7 Don't skimp on buying less fabric by ignoring the pattern matching—you will regret this every time you close your drapes or shades.

8 Never make the drapes too short as you will spoil the whole effect. Drapery should just "break" on the floor or, in certain styles, even crumple onto the floor in a puddle.

9 Don't make the mistake of putting a blind in a recessed window as it will block out the light. Always put the blind on the wall above the recess.

10 Be careful when using trims on drapes or shades— sometimes you can "over trim." If you have a plain fabric it can be fun to overdo things but with printed fabrics generally less is more.

2

Essentials

Introduction to essentials...

Choosing your drapery system...
In some cases there will be few options when it comes to choosing the type of drapes you want and what support system to have, but in others the possibilities are endless. Use this section to work out what will be the best choice in any given scenario.

Poles

Drapery poles are almost invariably fitted above the window recess, and they are designed to be on show. They are usually made of either wood or metal, but there is a wide range of finishes available in both types. The pole itself is generally rather plain, as the drapes have to slide along it, but decorative finials and the selection of drapery suspension system—hooks, rings, rope, eyelets—can make the design possibilities almost endless.

Poles can be used in both a traditional and a modern interior—there are design styles for both—and can be a major feature of the drapery design or just a background support system. When choosing your style of pole, be guided by the style of the drapery itself.

Tracks

In general, tracks are concealed—they are intended to be purely a support system for the drapes and a means to enable them to be closed. Heavy-duty tracks are made from metal, the lighter weight types are plastic. Make sure you have a suitable type, as drapery can be surprisingly heavy.

Some tracks are corded, which means that they have a system of pulleys and cords threaded up within the track and coming down at one side that allow the drapes to be opened and closed by pulling on a cord, rather than tugging the drape itself. Some of these corded systems are even motorized—essential for very large and heavy drapes, such as stage or cinema curtaining.

Covered lathes

A covered lathe is a flat length of wood that is covered in fabric and fixed to the front of a drapery track to conceal the track itself and its workings. It should be wide enough to hide the track, but does not need to be as deep nor as dressy as a pelmet or a valance. They are only used when a pelmet or valance is not suitable for some reason—either because of the type of window or door, or because the style of drapery does not need a dressy heading.

Covered lathes are not required on dress drapes that meet in the center to totally cover the track, but are a nice touch on drapery that does close, as they hide the expanse of track between the two drapes when they are open.

Panel glides

In a panel glide system, the panels hang flat without any fullness and glide as a unit over the window. If the opening size requires more than one panel, the panels can be staggered on the track so they stack up to just one panel width at the side. There is generally a limit of about 32 ft (10m) to the maximum opening width that can be accommodated, while the width of each individual panel is dictated by the width of the fabric available.

Like drapes, panels can be operated by hand—usually by means of a draw rod—with a cording system or by a motor. Panels are a great way to show off a spectacular fabric, as the details of the design are not lost within many folds of fabric.

Bay windows

Bay windows are the focal point of any room, as they are often large and let in the light, giving a great feeling of space. When you have a bay window in a room you will generally find there is another straight window in the room that should have the same style and fabric. A bay window can have two to six drapes depending on the size of the window. If there is a window seat in the bay it would be better to have functional Roman shades and have dress drapes either side.

Drapery fittings

The heading chosen for a the drapes will, to some extent, dictate what sort of fittings can be used. Simple gathered headings only need standard-size drapery hooks, but some of the more complex, tall headings need special longer hooks that will hold the weight of the heading upright and not allow it to droop.

Drapery rings come in a range of types and finishes to match the pole they are to be teamed with. Some rings are designed to be used with hooks, others have clips on the base that just clip onto the drapes.

Tabs and ties are generally made in the same fabric as the drapes, but can be made in a contrast color or replaced with ribbon or rope for a different look. Browse through the heading pages in this chapter to see a host of different ideas.

Valances

Valances are soft and made of fabric and have the same sort of heading as a set of drapes. In many ways they are a drape in miniature, but are not intended to close—instead they stay fixed in place to hide the fixings and the top of the drapes.

If drapery is to have a valance the drapes themselves should have a simple heading, since this will be concealed—any more complex heading to complete the design should be used on the valance. Although valances are generally not used with a pelmet, this is by no means a rule—some more elaborate designs will use both.

Pelmets

A pelmet is usually a solid three-dimensional box, with a front and a return at either side, that is fixed above the window recess to cover the top of the drapes and all the fixings. In some cases the pelmet may be a flat board that is fixed across the window recess, if the drapes are hung within the recess and not face-fixed.

Pelmets can be covered in fabric to co-ordinate with the drapery, and they can be trimmed in the same way and with the same materials as the drapes. They can also be carved, polished or painted wood, or even finished to match the walls of the room.

Traditional poles and finials

There are some amazing carved poles and finials to be found, whatever the period of your house—from Colonial to Georgian. Choose a pole the correct thickness for the weight of your drapes, and remember that a pole that is too thin looks odd with long drapes; try to get the right balance.

If you choose a Candy Twist pole you will find the rings don't slide easily over the twist parts, so perhaps use this pole for dress drapes.

Your poles and finials can generally be stained to any color or even painted to tie in with your color scheme. If you are using wooden hold-backs, then don't forget to stain or paint them the same color as the pole and finials.

Ball

Provençal style

Reeded finial and pole

Fluted ball

Antique brass finial and pole

Wooden hand-carved finial

Trumpet finial in two colors of wood

Art Deco

Gilded wooden finial and pole

Inverted rib and cage

Early Victorian-style "spinning top"

Leaf and acorn

Minaret candy twist pole

Victorian scroll

Coronet with decorative pole

Ottoman

Contemporary poles and finials

Brushed steel poles suit the sleek lines of minimalist drapes, especially in loft-style apartments. There are plenty of unusual shapes to choose from, but I have selected a few that I use constantly. I like to keep the pole and finial as plain as possible so as not to distract from the drapery design or the fabric—the simpler the better as far as I am concerned. There are double poles on the market now and this gives a much cleaner look when you have voile (sheer) drapes behind the main drapes, since you don't have to have tracking behind the pole. I use the black iron poles for country houses as they blend in beautifully with rustic interiors.

NOTE: If the pole is longer than 10ft (3m) you will need a center bracket. Buy a good-quality metal pole then it won't rust. Otherwise, varnish a cheaper one with a yacht varnish to keep it from rusting.

 Steel spire

 Wooden "bamboo" ball

 Steel ribbon ball

Iron button

Iron ball

Iron knot

Cage and ball

Shepherd's crook

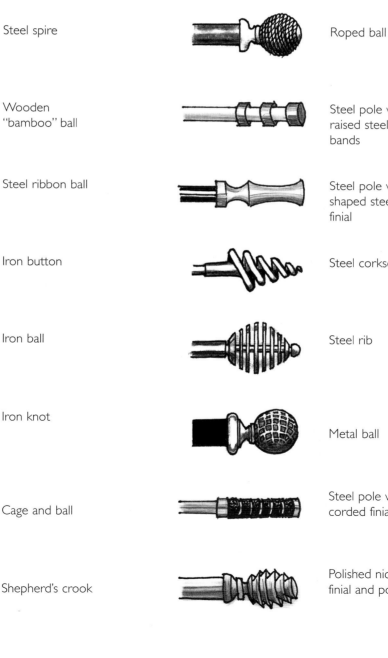

Roped ball

Steel pole with raised steel bands

Steel pole with shaped steel finial

Steel corkscrew

Steel rib

Metal ball

Steel pole with corded finial

Polished nickel finial and pole

Modern tracking systems

There are quite a few very good modern tracking systems to be found on the market these days. A selection of the best types are shown here. Also some manufacturers have finally sorted out a solution to the drama of having a drapery pole in a bay window—and about time too.

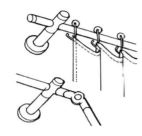

1   Stainless steel roller line pole. Can also be used for bay windows.

2   Stainless steel flat pole system—can be bent to form a return.

3   Tension wire system used from wall to wall. You can now have a "long span" wire (ask your manufacturer for information on this).

4   Stainless steel pole. Can be used with tension wire for secondary drapes.

5   Steel or iron arm used for recessed windows or room dividers.

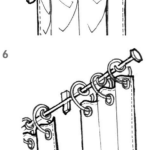

6   Various metal spiral rings—use for drapes with eyelet hole headings.

Tips

Be warned when using any of these systems—always read the manufacturer's instructions carefully.

Wire tracking can be used to hang lightweight drapes from wall to wall, within reason of course (see diagram 3).

Wire tracking is also useful when hanging drapes in a recessed window.

When ordering poles for a bay window always be sure the diagram is correct (see page 33).

Double poles are wonderful—now you can have lightweight voile drapes behind your main ones without two lots of tracking or a pole combined with tracking, which can be very messy.

Steel or iron arms are useful in dormer windows or cottage windows that are recessed.

Steel poles for bay windows

ALWAYS CHECK AND DOUBLE CHECK your diagram and dimensions before ordering these poles, as they cannot be altered once they are made and they are quite expensive.

Modern stainless steel poles can be made to fit any bay or difficult window. They are available in double poles too, which is wonderful for voiles and drapes at the same window.

There is only one drawback with these poles—you cannot have your drapes on pull cords (either manual or electric) so the drapes must be opened and closed by hand.

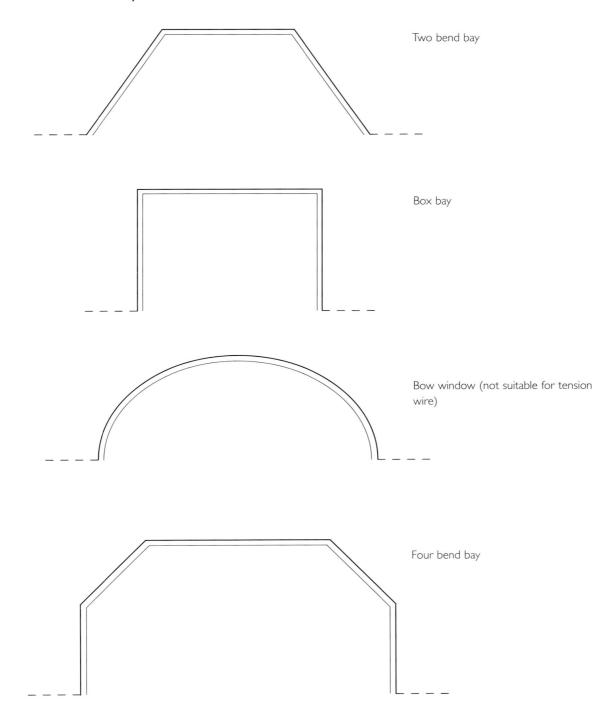

Two bend bay

Box bay

Bow window (not suitable for tension wire)

Four bend bay

Panel glide system

This is a relatively new system and it brings a totally new dimension to a room. Panels work really well in the home as well as in an office.

The tracking is fixed onto the ceiling or onto the wall and the panels hang straight down, without any fullness like drapes. They are a wonderful way to show off a large print, which would normally be lost in the folds of drapery.

The panel glide is available as either hand, cord or electrically operated—the hand-operated ones are pulled with an aluminum draw rod. When the panels are connected, which is required for hand as well as electrically operated types, the leading panel pulls the other panels along in sequence.

Panels can be specified to most reasonable sizes but anything over 19 ft (6m) wide would depend on the weight of the fabric and the manufacturer you are using. The maximum length is generally 32 ft (10m).

The panel fold is a motorized system, which can be operated by a fixed wall switch or even remote control. Panel folds are suitable for applications up to 16 ft (5m) wide and 10 ft (3m) drop. This type of panel can be hung rather closer to the ceiling than the sliding panel system.

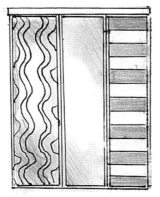
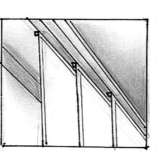

Here are a few sketches of panels, which show how versatile the panels are.

Two panels can be operated in the same way as drapes or can open to one side only.

A single panel in translucent voile- that can close either way.

Panels can be used as "doors" in front of a wardrobe or messy area like a child's toy closet.

Panels are best if the windows are very wide.

Basic drapery headings

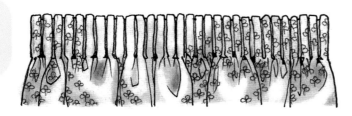

Regis or Pencil pleat

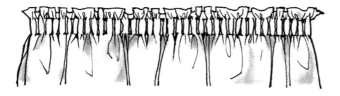

Unstructured

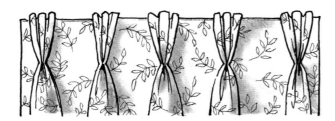

Triple pinch pleat or French pleat

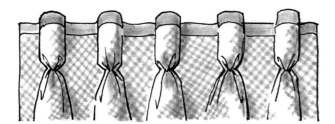

Goblet or Tulip

Unstructured with stand

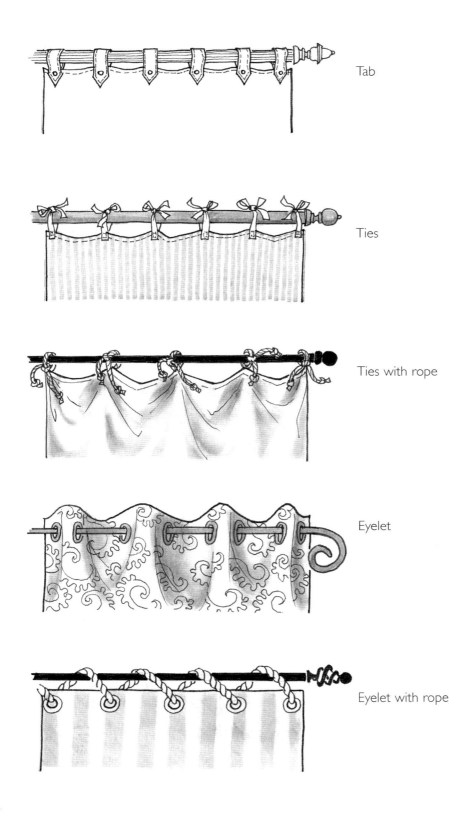

Tab

Ties

Ties with rope

Eyelet

Eyelet with rope

Basic drapery headings

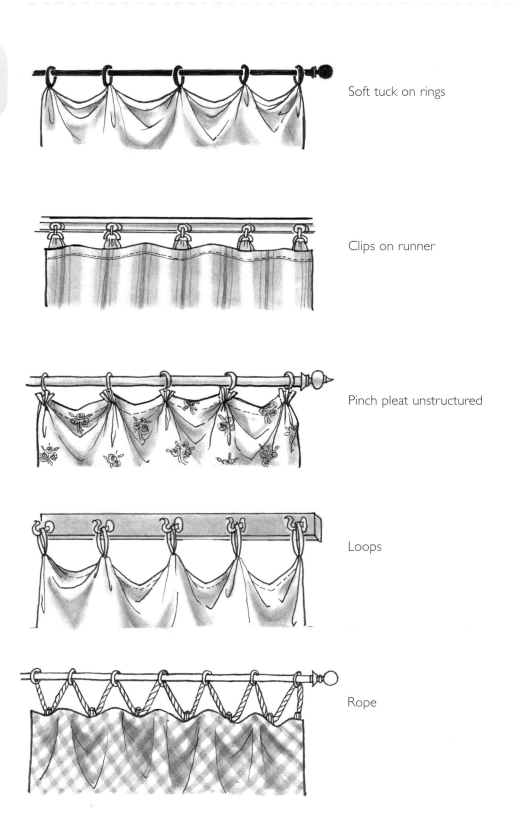

Soft tuck on rings

Clips on runner

Pinch pleat unstructured

Loops

Rope

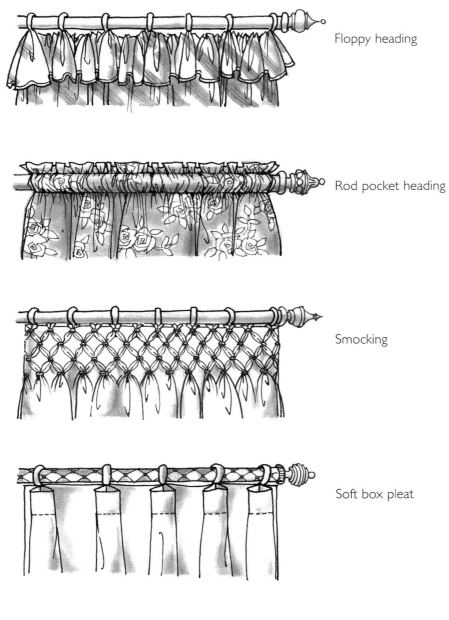

Floppy heading

Rod pocket heading

Smocking

Soft box pleat

Inverted pleat

Valances

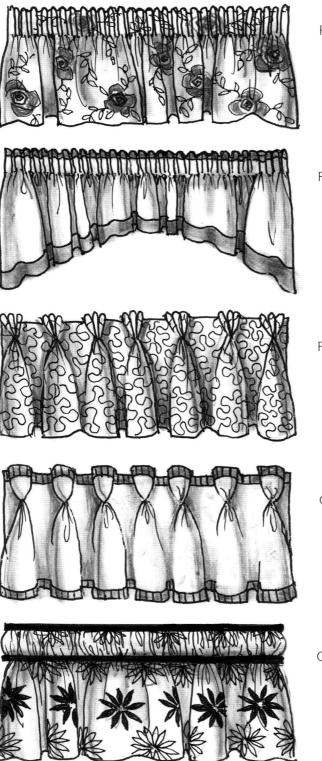

Regis or Pencil pleat

Pencil pleat with dropped sides

Pinch pleat

Goblet

Gathered

Tab

Tie

Regis or Pencil pleat with trim

Rod pocket heading with dropped sides

Draped

Pelmets

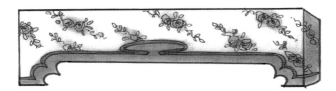

Fabric-covered pelmet with shaped base and contrast border

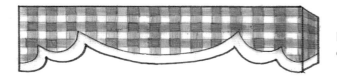

Fabric-covered pelmet with scalloped base and contrast border

Pelmet with Russian braid trim

Plain pelmet with braid and frogging detail

Shaped pelmet trimmed with tasselled fringing

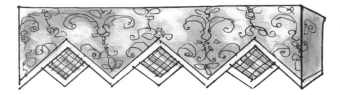

Chevron pelmet with two co-ordinating fabrics

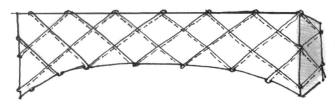

Fabric-covered pelmet with braid trim

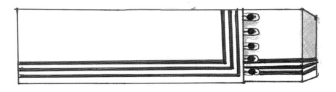

Fabric-covered pelmet cut-out design

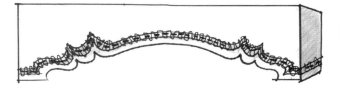

Fabric-covered pelmet with raised saddle-stitched lattice

Fabric-covered pelmet with Russian braid and button detailing

Hard carved pelmets

Simple pelmet with cornice and Greek key design

Wooden pelmet with cornice and fretwork scroll

Elaborate pelmet with egg-and-dart cornice and shaped base

Cornice pelmet with carved roses

Modern corniced pelmet with scalloped edge

Basketwork coronet with swags of roses and ribbons

Coronet, used above a bed

Hard carved pelmets and fretwork

Simple modern pelmet with central cut-out detail

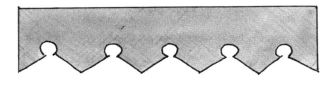

Plain pelmet with repeated chevron cut-out detail

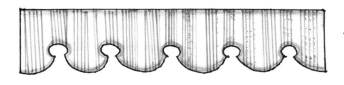

Wallpaper-covered pelmet with scalloped cut-out base

Simple fretwork pelmet

Elaborate fretwork pelmet

Wooden pelmet with repeating fretwork design

3

Finishing Touches

Introduction to finishing touches...

Adding that final touch...
Sometimes a fairly plain drapery design can be transformed, just by adding that one, perfect trim or the ideal tie-back. This chapter is designed to give you some ideas on how you can make your curtains look just that little bit more special.

Braids and ribbons

Braids and ribbons are the simplest and easiest trim you can add to a curtain design, but the effects you can achieve are stunning. Braids come in all designs, colors and styles, so you are sure to find the perfect one for your curtain. Russian braid is so versatile and easy to form into interesting shapes—the possibilities are almost endless!

Ropes and tassels

Ropes were traditionally often used as an extra design feature on curtains with swags and tails, but now they can be a decorative detail in themselves. Trim manufacturers make a standard range of ropes—many co-ordinated with matching tassels and trims—but can also make up colorways to order.

Tassels can be added alone or as the finishing touch to a length of rope. Again, they come in standard colorways to match other trims, or can be made up in special colors to match your fabric exactly.

Fringe and beaded trims

Fringe trim is created by weaving braid so that it has loops of yarn hanging downward from the base, and the lengths of fringe can be left in loops or sometimes trimmed into single strands. Bullion fringe has uncut loops twisted together to look like single strands, and is a particularly heavy, traditional type of fringe.

Beaded trims have beads or crystals that are either suspended from lengths of ribbon trim or threaded onto the loops of a fringed braid. This type of trim is ideal to add a touch of sparkle at the window.

Tie-backs and hold-backs

Tie-backs are lengths of fabric or rope that tie the drapes back against the wall and away from the window opening when they are not in use. They can be trimmed to match the drapes, and this chapter gives you plenty of ideas.

Hold-backs are solid metal or wood knobs or hooks that are fixed to the wall. When the drapes are drawn back it can be caught behind the hold-back to hold it in position. Both tie-backs and hold-backs can be used to keep dress drapes permanently in place.

Plain and trimmed

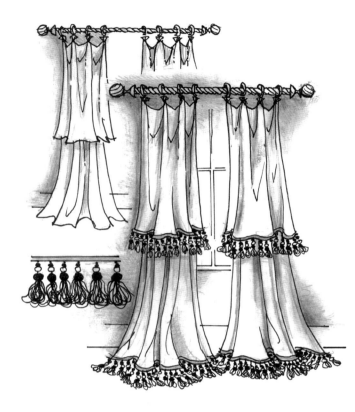

Adding a luxurious trim like this
can transform plain drapes.

Emphasize the unusual shape of this
design with a simple beaded fringe.

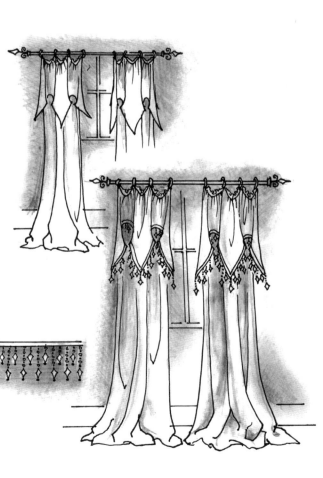

Trim

Finishing
Touches

Decorative
braid

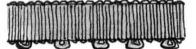

Grosgrain
braid

Single
edged
picot

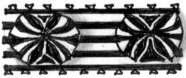

Pleated
ribbon
braid

Swirl motif
on grosgrain
ribbon

Striped
braid

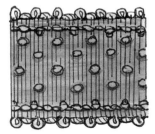

Jacquard
border

Picot ribbon
with beaded
edge

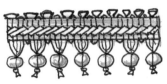

Delicate glass beaded
fringe

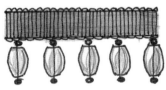

Picot
beaded
fringe

Novelty glass
beaded fringe

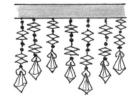

Crystal and
silk beaded
fringe

Venetian-style
beaded fringe

 Gimp

 Looped fan edge with tassels

 Picot ribbon

 Onion tassel fringe

 Rope

Neo-classical hanger fringe

Flanged rope

Bullion fringe with bead hangers

 Looped fan edge

Bullion fringe

 Twisted loop fringe

 Tufted fringe

 Fan edge

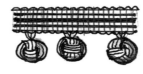 Striped braid with knotted pom poms

51

Trim

Bow braid
woven tape

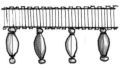

Lozenge
fringe

Tufted braid in
fine hand-woven
yarns

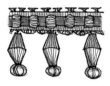

Lantern
hanger
fringe

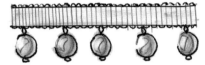

Glass-beaded
fringe

18th-century
tassel fringe

Pear-drop
beaded fringe
on gimp

Butterfly
beaded
fringe

Shell chip
fringe

Bauble
hanger
fringe

Pebble bead fringe

Novelty hanging
ropes used as
decoration on
curtains or
accessories

A kind of "key
tassel" with a
bauble instead of
a tassel

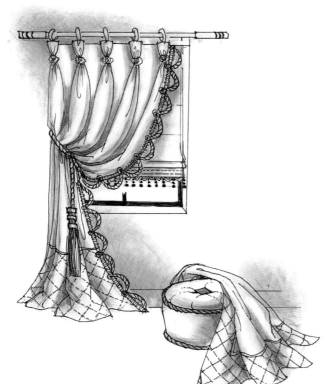

A quilted hem on the drape and
throw, plus a wonderful looped
trim on the leading edge of the
drape.

By adding trim to your other soft
furnishings, as shown here, you add
a touch of professionalism.

Trim

A contemporary collection of simple woven braids and fringes, all combining a wrapped technique and style. The two tie-backs offer a less formal design with a more modern approach.

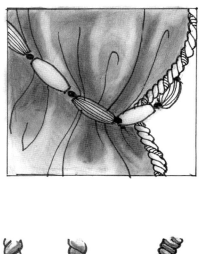

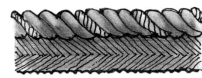

Flanged rope

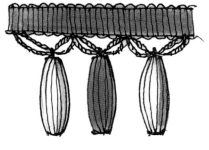

Double cut fringe

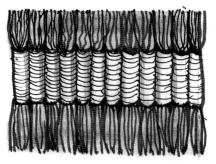

Cut fringe

Unusual tie-backs

Picot ribbon with covered lozenges

Picot ribbon with lozenge-style covered shape

Elegance and glamor—a combination of crystal and glass trim for an opulent interior. Swarovski crystals delicately woven into silk braid headings and hand-twisted cords.

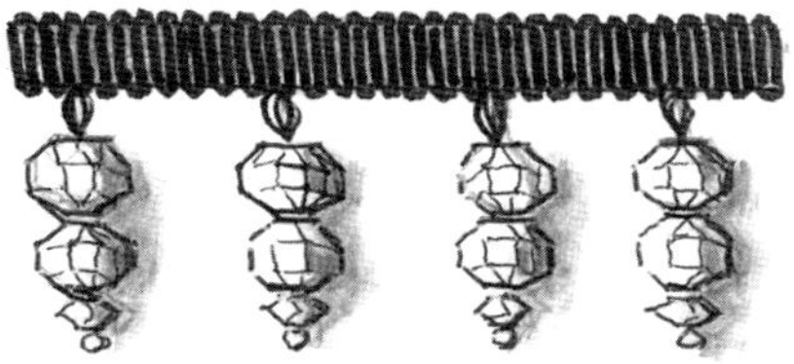

Crystal drop fringe

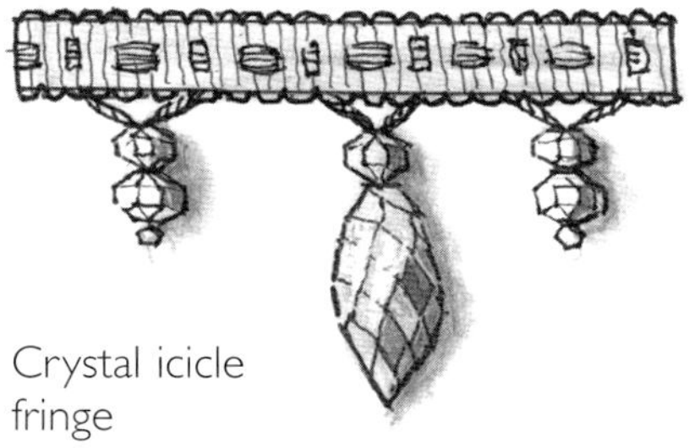

Crystal icicle fringe

Crystallia tie-back

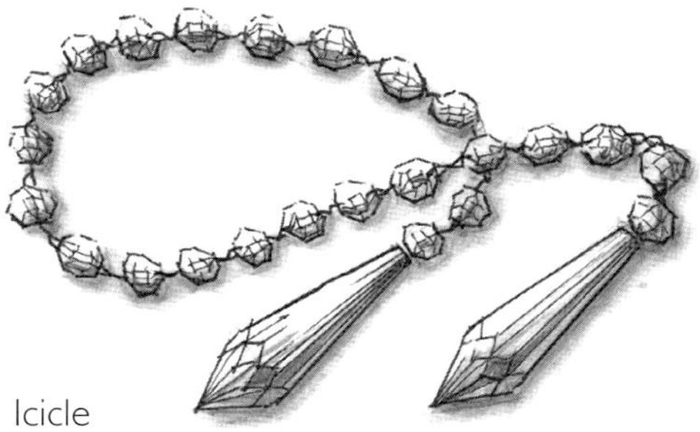

Icicle hangers

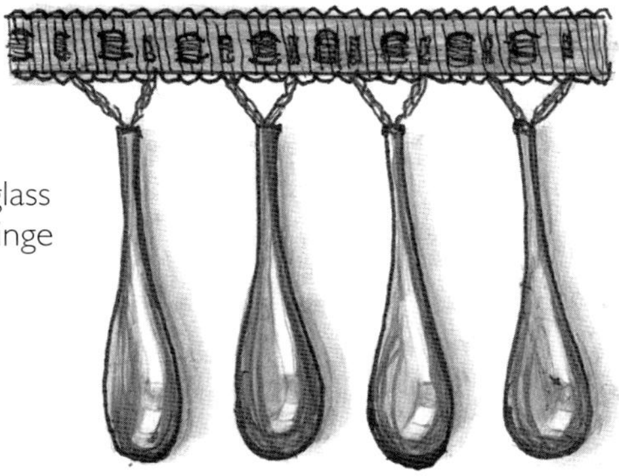

Murano glass lantern fringe

Murano glass tie-backs

Bead and crystal hangers

Beaded trim

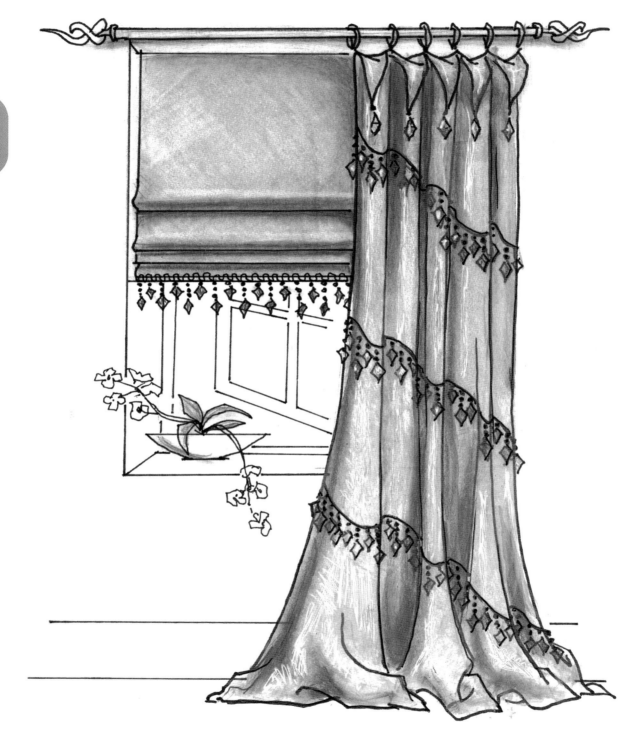

This Roman shade and dressed drape are both edged
with a stunning crystal trim.

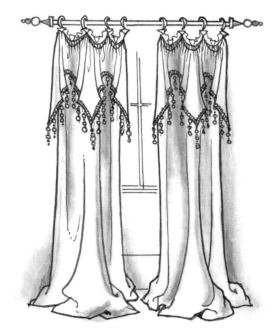

Unstructured curtain with beaded trim.

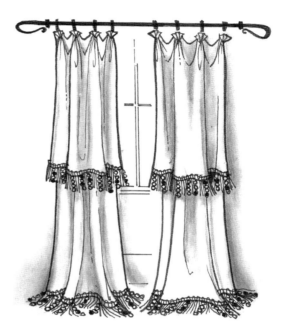

Two-tiered drapes with beaded fringe.

One-sided drape with delicate crystal trim.

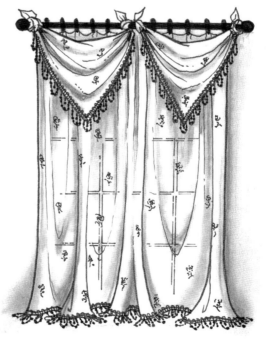

Printed voile with looped beading on the hem.

Ribbons and braids

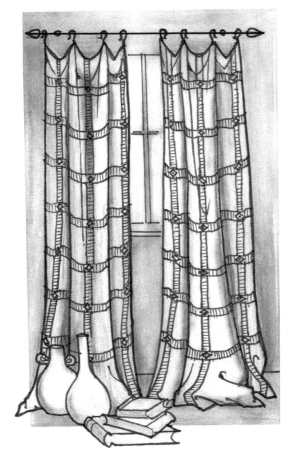

Hessian ribbons machined onto the fabric in a simple grid.

Fringed heavy wool curtains with a wide Jacquard ribbon border.

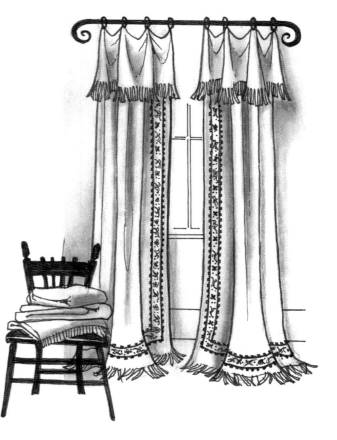

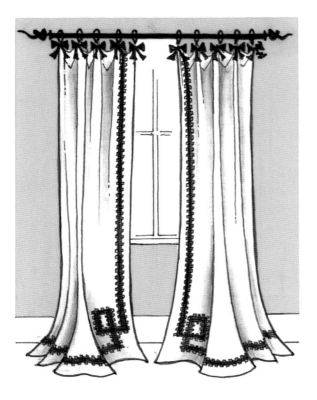

A simple picot ribbon machined along the leading edge and forming a square "knot" design in the bottom corner. The heading ties are the same ribbon.

Sewing picot ribbons on vertically visually adds height to the drapes.

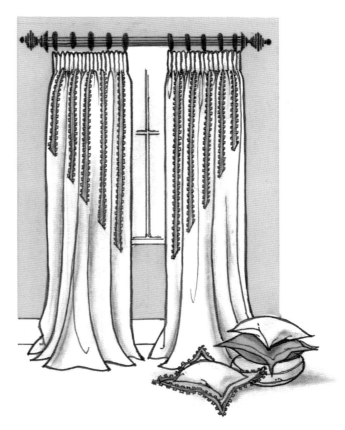

Tasselled trim

Plain drapes with a
gathered valance...

... are transformed by adding tassel fringing to the
valance and rope to the leading edges of the drapes.

60

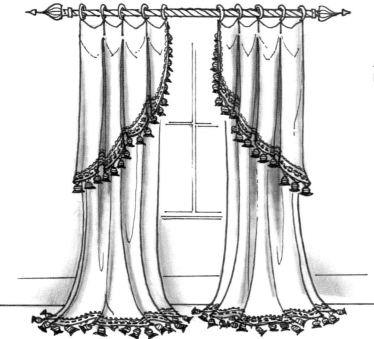

Accentuate the shape of this design by adding unusual fringing.

Valance with a slotted heading and edged with tassels, over dressed drapery and an Italian-strung drape.

Mixing trim

To achieve a unique look, try using wide ribbon as a base and adding various other trims.

Finishing Touches

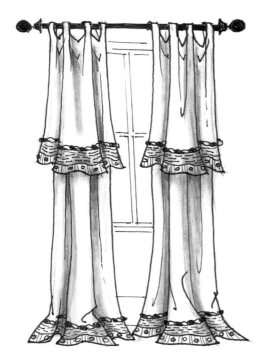

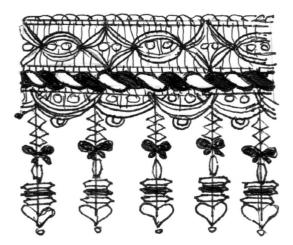

Woven braid, rope and beaded fringe.

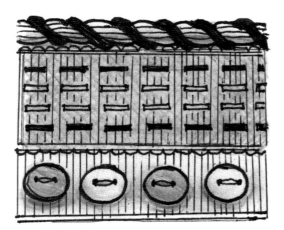

Rope, woven ribbon and buttons on picot.

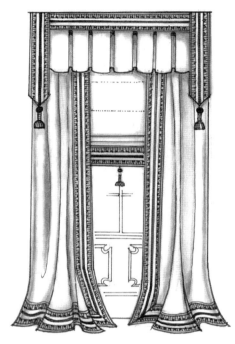

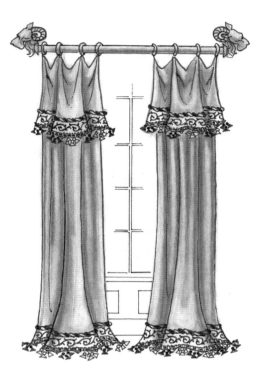

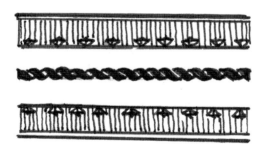

Grosgrain ribbon, picot ribbon and rope.

Rope, Jacquard ribbon and tassel fringe.

Tie-backs

Cord, loop and beaded tie-backs offer a less formal alternative to the formal tassel tie-back. Most trim ranges include these, to co-ordinate with the other trims.

Contemporary tie-backs

Contemporary bauble tie-backs—covered wooden molds are an alternative to tassel tie-backs.

Wrapped and bound tassel tie-backs in a contemporary style.

Elegant tassel decorations—crystal, bead and lozenge designs.

Traditional tie-backs

Traditional decorative tie-backs with beaded and tassel hangers.

Casual, less formal tie-backs.

Tie-backs influenced by historical designs.

Fabric tie-backs

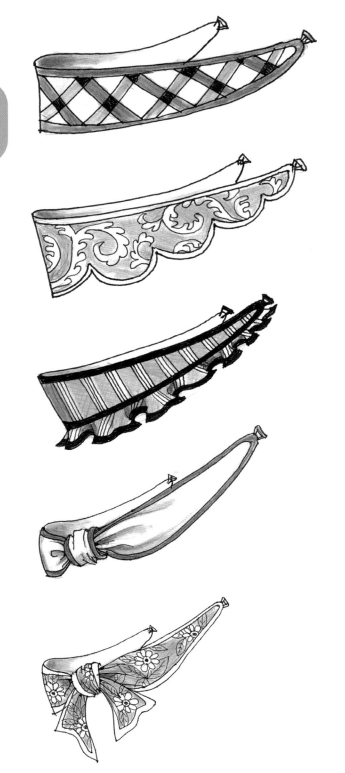

Simple crescent

Scalloped edge

Crescent with bias-cut ruffle

Casual knotted crescent

Tied crescent

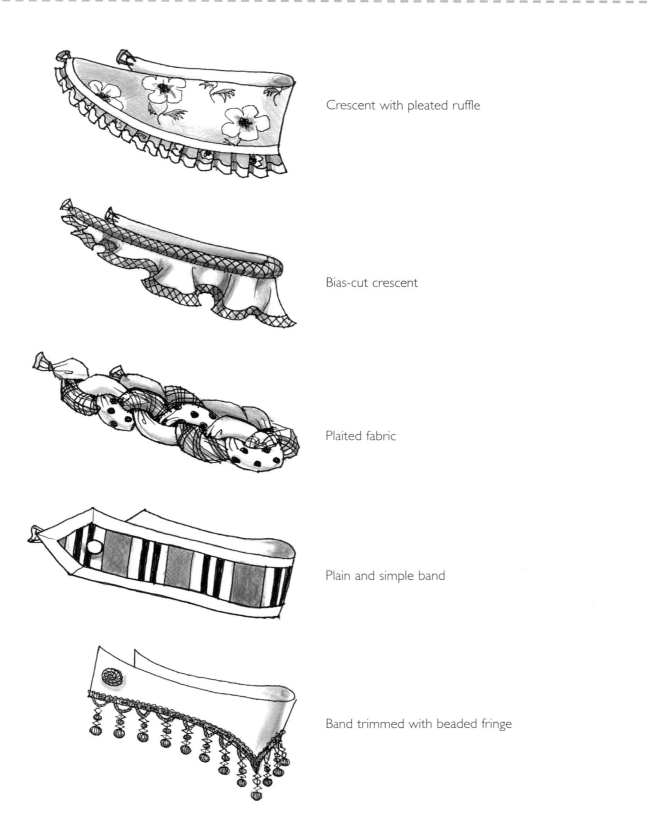

Crescent with pleated ruffle

Bias-cut crescent

Plaited fabric

Plain and simple band

Band trimmed with beaded fringe

Hold-backs

These "hold-backs" are designed to neatly hold back the drapes to let in more light.

"Ombres" or "embraces" gather up the drapery.

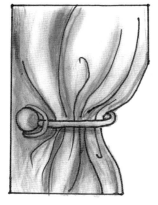
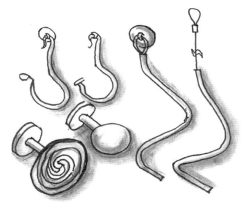

Modern metal swing-arm hold-backs, used for voile or sheer drapes.

4

Basic Headings

Introduction to basic headings...

Choosing a heading...
The heading you choose for your drapes will often set the style for the whole design, so it's worth taking some time to get it right. Here we look at the different headings and how to achieve them, and on the following pages you will see the headings in action on drapes, a valance, or a pelmet.

Pencil pleat

Regis heading, also sometimes called a pencil pleat heading. A regis heading tape is sewn on near the top of the drapes and the strings on the tape are pulled to form a neat row of single pencil pleats right across the top.

Triple pinch pleat

The triple pinch pleat is also sometimes called the French pleat. It can be made using heading tape but for the best effect use drapery buckram between the layers at the top of the drapes. Pockets are formed on the face of the drapes and are then pinched together to form either double or triple pleats.

Floppy

Cut the drapes longer, adding double the amount you want them to flop over into a ruffle at the top, plus another 1 in (2.5 cm) to go under the tape. Turn over the fabric and the lining to the back of the drapes and sew on a narrow heading tape to cover the raw edge. Pull the strings to the required width, then turn over the ruffle.

Goblet

This heading is sometimes called a tulip heading. Like the pinch pleat, it can be done with a heading tape but is best formed in the same way as described for pinch pleats. The tops are then opened up to form a goblet, with wadding or a separate curl of buckram inserted to maintain the goblet shape.

Rod pocket

The rod pocket heading is also sometimes called a pocket heading, or a slotted heading in the UK. This is a pocket or slot formed across the top of the drapes, sometimes with an upstand for a more decorative effect. The slot should be a bit bigger than the pole so that the drapery slides onto it easily.

Inverted pleat

This is a very casual heading, a simple inverted pleat caught with stitches at the top of the drapes to hold the pleat in place. It can have buckram for a stiff top but I prefer to keep it soft and less formal.

Box pleat

A square pleat at intervals across the heading. Work out how many box pleats you need for the width of each drape. Make sure you allow the same amount of fabric under the pleat or the drapery will not fall correctly. Pin the pleats in place and gently press the top only. Machine or hand sew the pleat across the base. For a more formal heading use buckram. This heading can only be used for static drapery, as they will not draw back from the window.

Tab

The tabs are made out of strips of fabric, looped over with the raw ends placed between the drapes and the lining at the top and sewn in place. The tabs should be bigger than the pole so that they slide along to open and close easily.

Unstructured

The unstructured heading is a dainty heading, which is best for thin delicate fabrics such as voile or lawn. Use a heading tape that is sewn onto the top of the drapes; when the strings are pulled it gathers into narrow informal pleats.

Pinch pleat unstructured

Just take a small pinch of fabric and sew to a ring at equal intervals along the top of the drapes, then thread the rings onto a pole. No buckram—keep this very soft.

Eyelet

For people sewing at home, the best way to achieve eyelets is to use heading tape stitched in place, then cut the holes by hand and clip the eyelets together from either side of the hole. The alternative is to hire or buy a rather expensive manual hole punch or eyelet machine. Alternatively, you might find a workroom who can punch the eyelets in for you for a small charge.

When the eyelets are in place, they are then simply threaded onto a pole, or rope is looped through each and over the pole in between.

Clip

The clips are attached to the bottom of the rings that slide onto the drapery pole, or to a runner system. The top of the drapes should have some thickness so that the clip has something to fix to—make sure your fabric is not too heavy as often clips will not take much weight. They are great for sheers and lightweight, unlined cottons.

Ties

These are similar to tabs, but the ties are two separate strips of fabric that just tie over the top of the pole. Instead of fabric ties you can use short lengths of rope stitched to the top of the drapes at intervals.

Basic headings

One-sided Italian-strung drape with huge looped
trimming.

Pencil

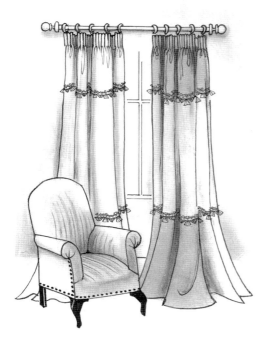

Insets of fabric are edged with a simple tassel trim.

Short drapes should only be used when there is no alternative.

A one-sided drape is a great solution for a deeply recessed window.

Basic headings

A triple pleat heading adds interest to the simple lines of these drapes.

Use a contrast lining, pulled back and hooked onto the tie-backs.

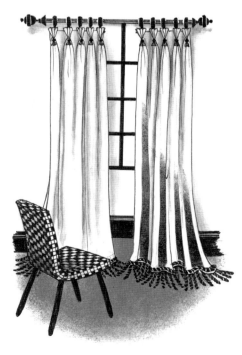

Emphasize the triple pinch pleats with tiny tassels at the base of each set.

Pinch pleated

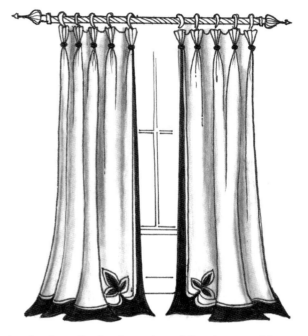

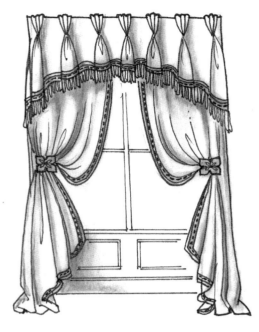

Appliqué on the leading edge of the drapes adds a touch of drama.

This classic design has a goblet-pleated valance and the drapes are pulled softly over hold-backs.

Italian-strung drapes are ideal for a very formal setting. Ropes and tassels add extra interest.

Basic headings

A simple, classic goblet heading.

Goblet

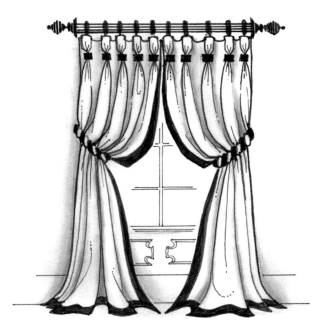

Large square buttons at the base of each goblet match the color of the contrast trim on the leading edge and hem of the drapes.

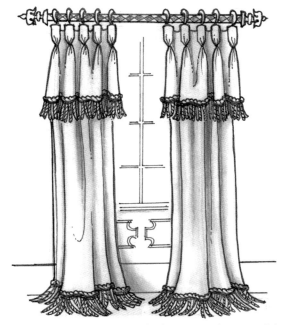

Heavy bullion fringing works best on a heavyweight fabric, such as wool tweed.

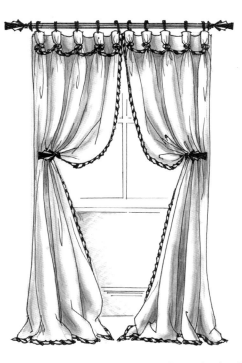

Two-tone rope looks spectacular along the leading edge of the drapes and knotted under the goblets.

Basic headings

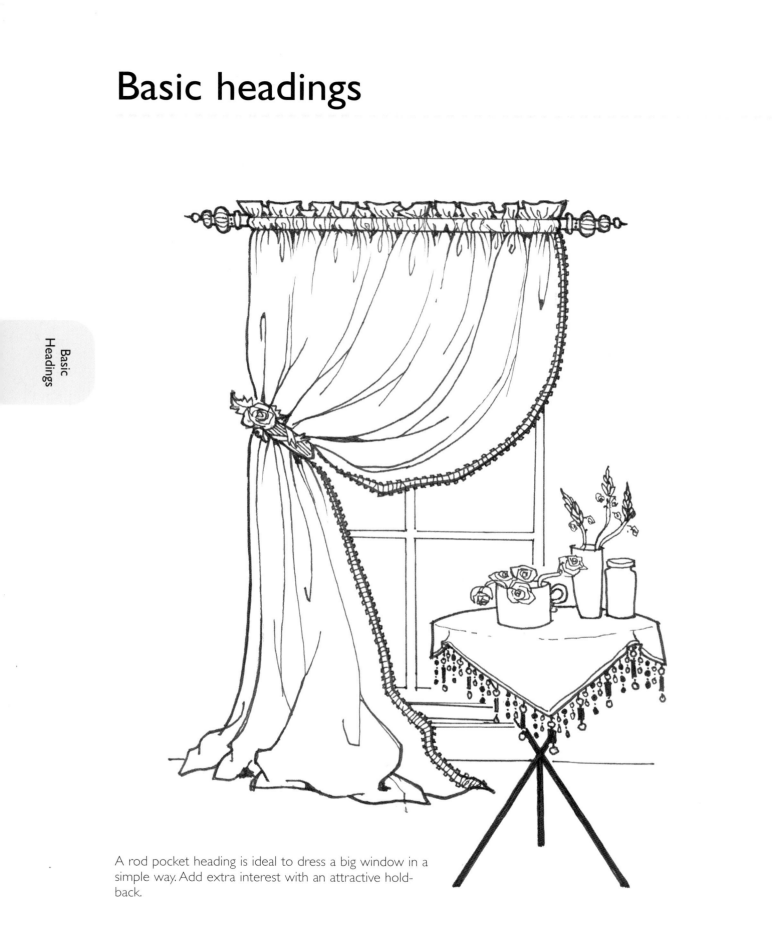

A rod pocket heading is ideal to dress a big window in a simple way. Add extra interest with an attractive hold-back.

Slotted/pocket

Double drapes on a double rail—and the over-drapes are lined in the same contrast fabric used for the under-drapes.

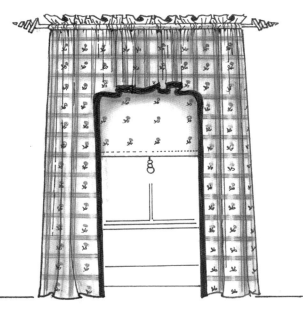

This shaped dress drapery frames the window. The shade behind it is functional.

The long dress drapes are not intended to close. The voile café curtain is trimmed with bands of matching ribbon.

Basic headings

Here, the contrast border is repeated along the bottom edge of the valance and enhanced with an appliqué design at the center of the window.

A wide Jacquard ribbon bordering the leading edge and deep fringing on the hem give a different look.

Inverted pleat

A wide contrast border all around the edges creates a
dramatic outline.

Silk drapes are given an extra touch of luxury with a
deep ruffled border.

The edge of this Italian-strung portière drape is
highlighted with wide braid.

Basic headings

Basic plain tab drapes are simple and elegant.

Tab

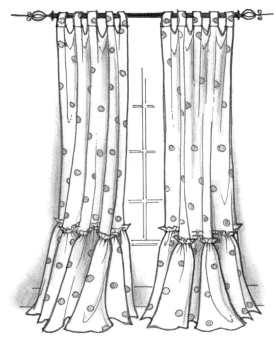

A deep ruffle in matching or contrasting fabric creates interest at the base of the drapes.

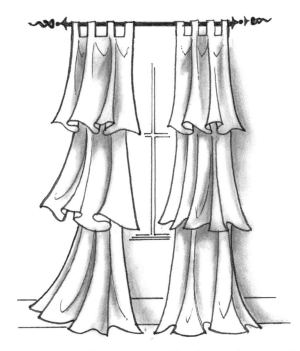

Three-tiered ruffle cut on the bias for a soft, romantic look.

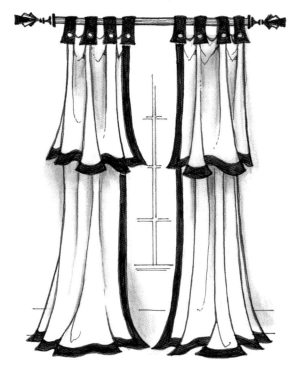

Buttoned tabs in the same dramatic contrast fabric used for the borders of this two-tier drapery.

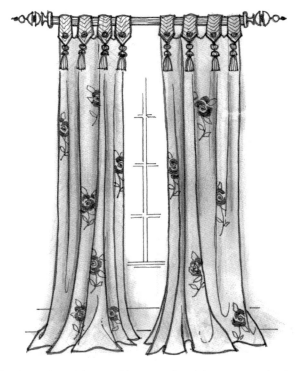

Burlap tabs with matching tassels add extra emphasis to the heading.

87

Basic headings

Inset contrast bands set on the diagonal for extra flair. Bias-cut fabric hangs beautifully.

Large bold prints need large bold details—such as this deep ruffle.

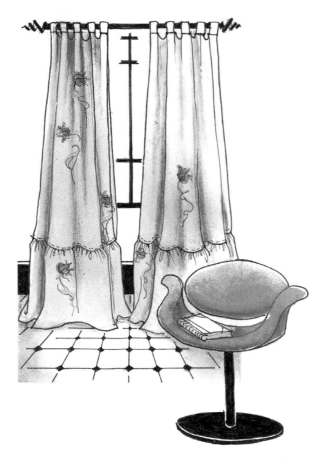

Tab

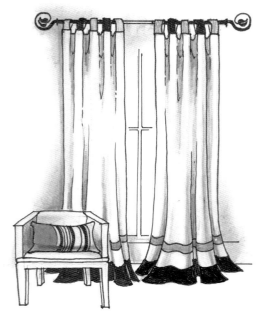

A simple design is given wow-factor by the triangular over-hanging with tassels and a deep bullion fringe at the hem.

Double contrasting bands at the hem are echoed by the alternating tabs at the heading.

Box pleated and buttoned tabs give a smart tailored look.

Jute fringing is matched with burlap tabs for a fully co-ordinated design.

Basic headings

The casual crumpled look of an unstructured heading looks great in linen.

Unstructured

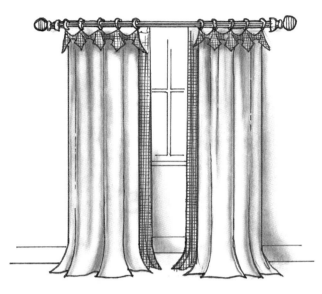

Double drapes, with a tiny check pattern on the under-drapery that is echoed in the "Robin Hood" turnovers at the top of the over-drapes.

A valance cut on the bias hangs in soft folds that complement the unstructured look.

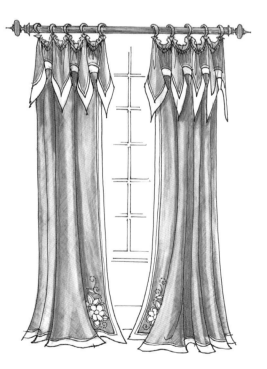

The handkerchief points of the skirt are emphasized by the contrast border, which is repeated along the leading edge of the drapes. Appliqué adds extra style.

Two-tiered drapes with wide contrast bands will make a very tall window look shorter.

Basic headings

Eyelet drapery is very practical across alcove openings, creating an eye-catching panel of color when closed.

Double-sided drapes are hooked back to reveal the contrast lining. Here they hide unsightly computer equipment.

Eyelet

Two-tone fabric in a checkerboard pattern is set off with contrast saddle stitching.

For a truly rustic look, nothing can beat a burlap curtain.

Smart Russian braid on the leading edge and along the base of the valance evokes a military look.

Sailcloth drapes with lacing across the center give a nautical feel.

Basic headings

Absolutely no sewing required—just clip a lightweight
rug or blanket onto a pole.

Clip

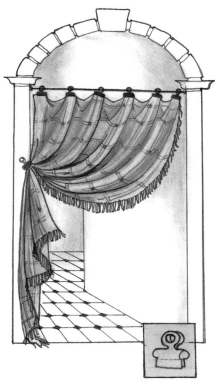

One-sided drapes are ideal for a portière. Emphasize the curve of the edge with fringing.

A simple panel clipped to a pole and pinned back at the center.

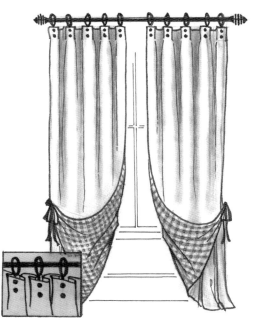

Black studs on box pleats echo the color of the iron pole. The drapes are pulled back and tied to reveal the stylish checked lining.

Basic headings

Tie-on headings and a deep ruffle on silk drapes give a
romantic look suitable for a bedroom.

Tie

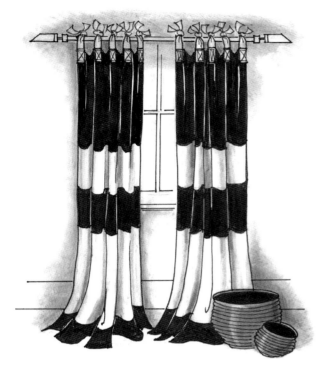

Heavily contrasting bands are very dramatic and the horizontal lines make a narrow window look wider.

A variation with zigzag bands instead of straight lines, making the drapes look long and elegant.

Diagonal lines of crystal trimmings add style and sparkle.

Using beaded string to tie the drapery to the pole creates an informal feel.

Basic headings

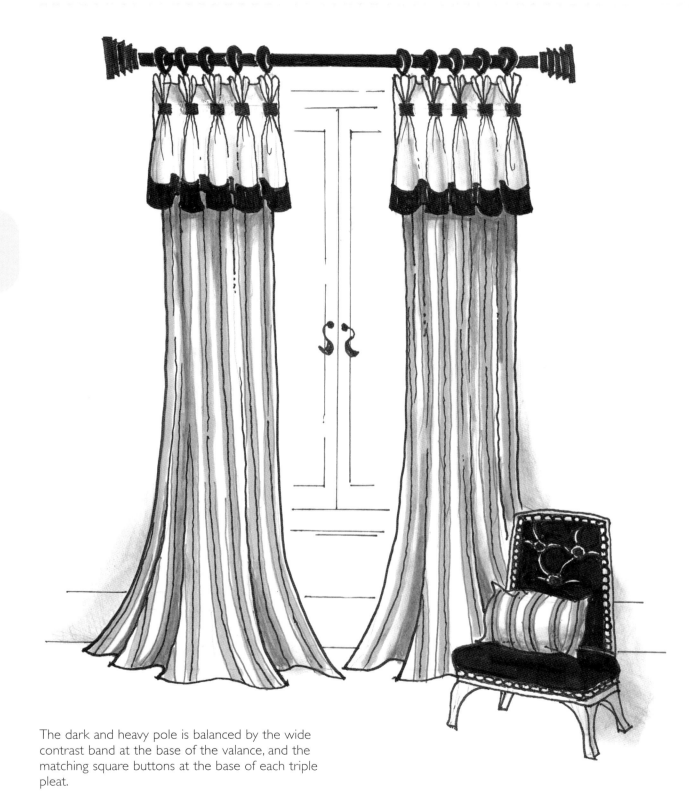

The dark and heavy pole is balanced by the wide
contrast band at the base of the valance, and the
matching square buttons at the base of each triple
pleat.

Soft valance

An unstructured clip-on valance creates a soft informal look.

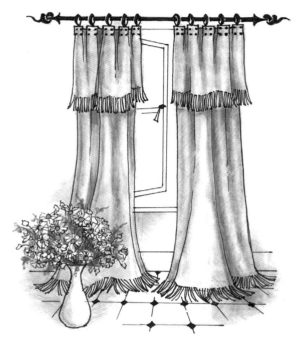

The box pleats at the top are attached to the rings with studs. Deep fringing on both hems is made of rough wool.

The deep crystal edging on the top skirt of this double drapery is at eye-level for maximum impact.

Valances

Studded box heading and valance edged with Russian braid.

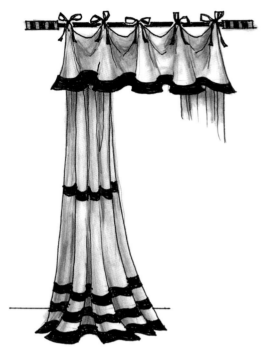

Contemporary steel pole with tie-on valance.

The wonderful bold print used for the valance is also the drapery lining.

Valances

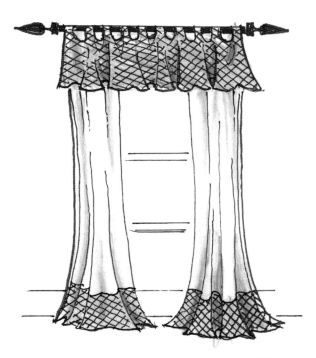

This valance is cut on the bias so it falls beautifully.

A simple valance made special by using a large cabbage rose print.

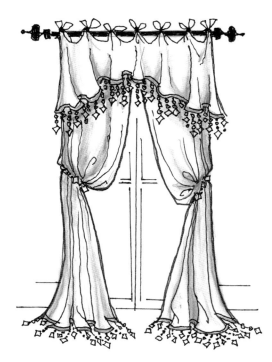

Plenty of beaded trim is wonderful for a bedroom.

Unusual spotted valance with a coordinated jet beaded trim.

Valances

A box-pleated heading on this gathered valance. It has
a pretty shape with the drop in the middle as well as at
the sides, and the drapery is lined in matching material.

Valances

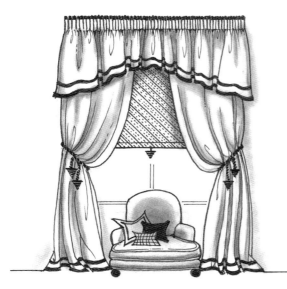

Pencil pleat valance with dropped sides, its classic shape emphasized with a double line of Russian braid.

A shaped pencil pleat valance with a bias-cut ruffle that gently flutes.

Draped valance with a deep bullion fringe.

Valances

Black and white rope trim to match the black and
white colorway of this dramatic spotted fabric. The
rope is added to show off this simple traditional shape.

104

Valances

A simple gathered heading on this valance with a stand. The valance has over-long droopy sides edged with a pretty looped fringe.

A double pleated valance with droopy sides, heavily trimmed with beads.

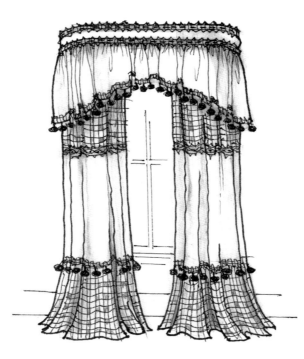

Valance co-ordinated with the center section of drapes with mixed fabrics, and trimmed with a matching bobble fringe.

Pelmets

A wonderful boldly spotted pelmet—but keep the main drapes plain.

Wide black braid on the pelmet and hem is echoed in the smart black buttons.

Russian braid is really easy to stitch on so you can create your own designs.

The colors of the wide striped pelmet are complemented in the plain drapes and border.

106

Pelmets

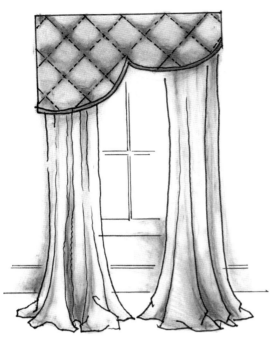

This unusual one-side, double-scallop pelmet is quilted.

Quilted pelmets look best in plain velvet, teamed with soft silk drapes.

Before cutting the fabric for this pelmet, make an accurate paper pattern of the design motif.

Huge flowers make a dramatic statement on this spectacular pelmet—team it with plain drapes.

5

Traditional and Modern Designs

Introduction to styles...

Choosing your style...
Sometimes fairly plain drapes can be transformed, just by adding that one, perfect trim or the ideal tie-back.

This chapter is designed to give you some ideas on how you can make your drapery look just that little bit more special.

Swags and tails

Swags and tails are an essential feature of many classic drapery styles—the swag is the sweeping drape of fabric across the top of the drapery head, the tail is the end of fabric that hangs down in graceful folds at the sides. Even the most simple swag and tails will add a touch of elegance to a drapery design, but there are hundreds of variations on the basic theme, some of them extremely elaborate.

Despite their classical roots, swags and tails have also been incorporated in modern designs—sometimes in quite eyecatching and unusual ways. Although usually a team, swags can be used without tails and tails without swags. Informal swags can be created just by draping lengths of fabric or a beautiful shawl across a drapery pole.

Contemporary

Modern designs tend to use simpler headings than the traditional designs, or to use entirely different ways of supporting the drapes: eyelet holes, rope, ties or tabs, for instance. Modern designs also sometimes combine elements in an unusual way, or use items that would not normally be considered for a window treatment, such as greenery, simple fabric panels or using voiles without over-drapes.

Although generally less elaborate than traditional drapes, contemporary drapery can still be very elegant and stylish. Dress drapes are not so often part of the design, but a modern design may still include two layers, perhaps with co-ordinating fabrics.

Classic styles

Traditional drapery designs range from simple but well-dressed to extremely elaborate. They don't necessarily need to have swags and tails; they may have a decorative pelmet or a draped valance, or just feature an elegant heading on a beautiful pole, while fringes, ropes and tassels are often part of the design.

It is also common to have more than one layer in a classic design. Since much of the appeal of a traditional design is in the beautiful way it is arranged, dress drapes—which can be left in their place—are often teamed with a secondary window covering that is functional: perhaps elaborate over-drapes over voiles, or an Italian-strung drape over some type of shade. The dress or over-drape should also be fully lined—a single layer of fabric will not hang elegantly.

Bay windows

Bay windows can be hard to design for—do you dress them as one unit, or as separate windows? If the bay has French windows it makes things even more complicated. Much will depend on how deep the bay is, how close its component windows are to each other and whether there is seating.

Both traditional and modern drapery designs will work on a bay – so ultimately the choice of design will depend on the style of the rest of the room. For a range of alternative ideas for a bay, see pages 132 to 137.

Italian stringing

These angled draperies with a straight hem line are a difficult treatment to make successfully. Italian stringing is a method of "stringing" or "opening" drapes in which the drapes are fixed at the top, so the only parts that move are the bottoms—these are pulled up by means of a cord or multiple cords attached to the back.

Because the heading is fixed in place, Italian-strung drapes are often the ideal solution for unusual window shapes— particularly if it's the shape of the window head that is the problem. They are also great as dress drapes, since they are not intended to close.

Voiles/sheers

Voiles have often been treated as unimportant—just there to obscure glass for privacy. However, modern voiles come in such a wide range of colors, designs and prints that they can make a statement all of their own. Voiles are often teamed with dress drapes, but can also be layered alone for a light window style. They are excellent if there is no need for the light to be obscured, as they will allow natural light to filter through.

Dress drapes

A dress drape is any drapery that is designed for show and not to actually close across the window. It doesn't necessarily have to be actually fixed in place so it cannot close—it is just a curtain that is not intended to do so, and so its design can be more elaborate. The way it is dressed at the window can also be more elaborate, as it does not have to be returned to position each time it is moved. Dress drapes are usually teamed with an alternative window treatment, either a shade, voiles or secondary drapes.

Swags and tails

Swags and tails in a highly patterned fabric accentuated
with ropes and tassels complement simple
unstructured drapes.

A traditional design teamed with a candy twist pole.

A simplified modern version of swags and tails.

Swags and tails combined with a carved pelmet and a one-sided Italian-strung drape.

Swags and tails used alone are a useful treatment for a round window.

Swags and tails

Traditional
and Modern
Designs

An elegant design with swags and tails edged with
beading and patterned voile under-drapery beneath
unstructured and softly placed over-drapes.

Traditional swags and tails edged with deep fringing.

Use a heavy fabric for this design, teamed with a heavy fringe.

A more modern version of swags and tails, with fabric gathered and draped from an upright finial at each end.

Traditional and Modern Designs

Swags and tails

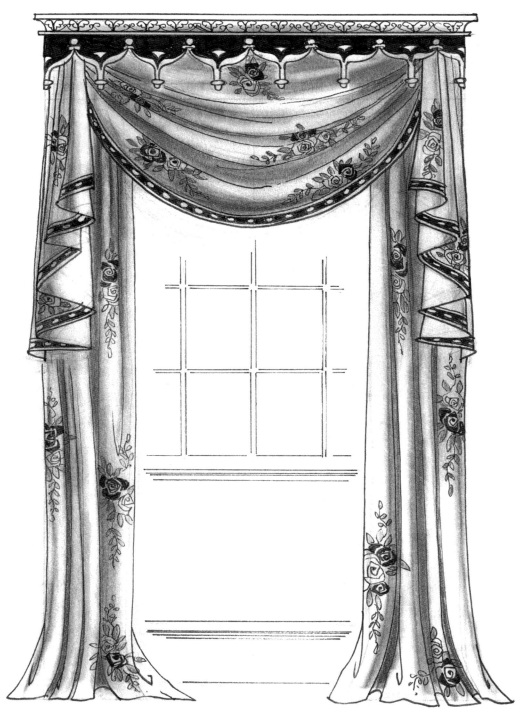

A classic design in which the bold braid edging
accentuates the curve of the swag and the meandering
folds of the tails.

Traditional
and Modern
Designs

Triple swags edged with a deep crystal fringe and highlighted with bold rosettes.

Heavy tweed trimmed with wool bullion fringe, ideal for a plain, bold interior.

Dressing a window recess just with swags and tails works well if there is no room for drapes.

Traditional

Carved roses on the pelmet with lots of hanging crystals and crystal trim to the swags.

A very formal design with a deep pelmet, swags and tails that should only be used if the ceilings are high.

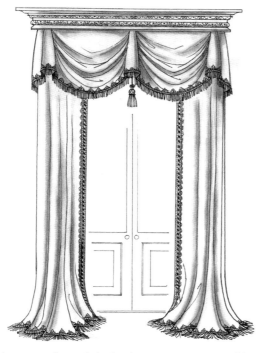

Another very formal design but a narrower and less elaborate pelmet means it can be used with lower ceilings.

A pretty carved pelmet and the Italian-strung drapery is edged with crystal beaded trim.

This simple but elegant design is lovely in a bedroom in soft pastel silk.

A scrolled carved pelmet. The under-drapes close, the over-drapes are dress drapes.

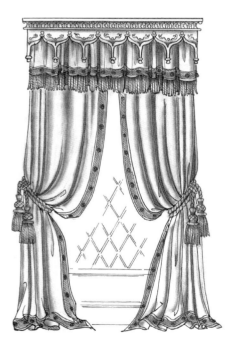

An elaborate carved pelmet and deep valance, suitable for a hisroric home.

This complicated heading is teamed with a simple printed voile.

Traditional

A single swag with tasseled ropes instead of tails.

Simple design in silk with a double swag and crystal trims, suitable for a bedroom.

A rod pocket heading like this is only suitable for dress drapes, as this drapery would not be able to open.

The studded, box-pleated heading gives this contemporary drapery design a traditional look.

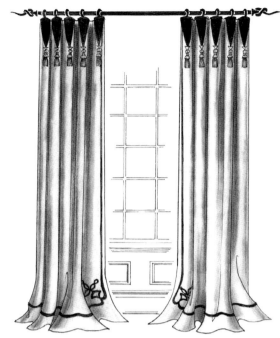

Contrasting goblet pleats across the heading, each trimmed with a tassel to finish.

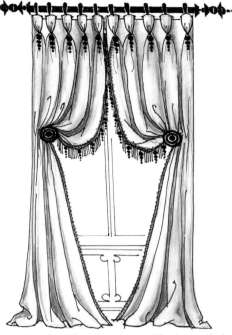

Elegant goblet headed drapery with dramatic jet beads on the base of the goblets and partially trimmed with jet fringing.

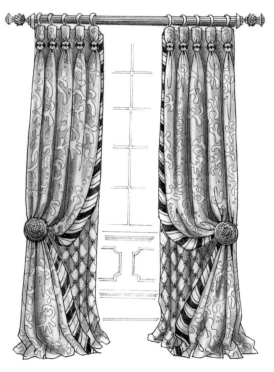

Here the main drapes are only dress drapes, but the under-drape does draw.

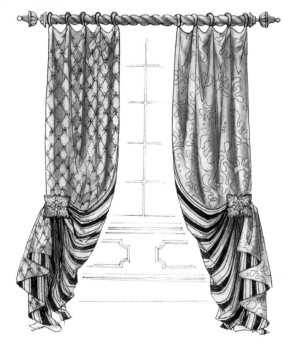

A different damask is used for each drape, but both are lined with a bold striped silk.

Traditional

In formal settings there are often two windows side-by-side—here is one way to treat them.

Twin windows can also be dressed with a drape each, but styled as a pair.

Draped pelmets always look dramatic, whether with one drape...

... or teamed with two drapes.

Modern

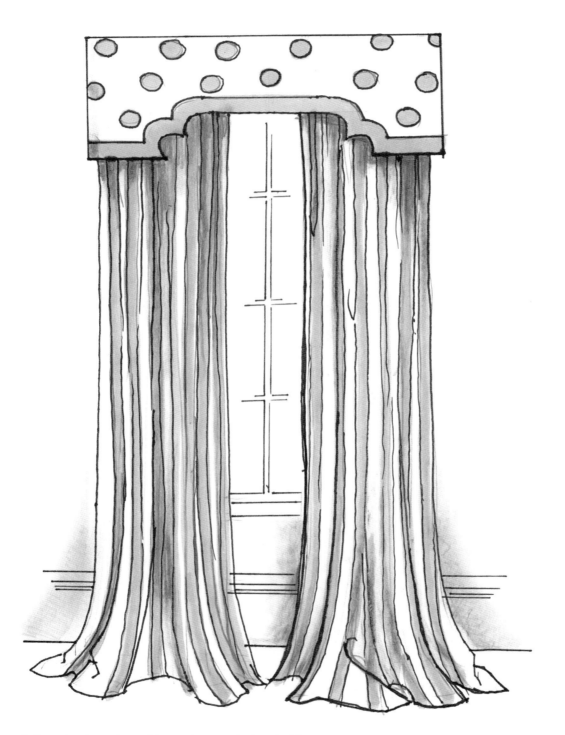

A formal pelmet, but with a twist—made in a bold spotted fabric and teamed with wide stripe drapes.

Modern

Traditional and Modern Designs

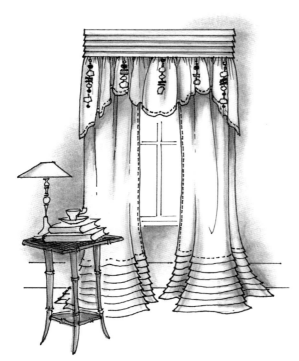

A versatile design because you can alter the look by changing the items hanging from the valance.

This valance has studded box pleats and a wide border top and bottom to accentuate its shape, which is echoed in the border at the hem of the drapes.

Plain and simple valance, but with a contrast rope trim to add interest.

A bias-cut valance falls in soft, attractive folds.

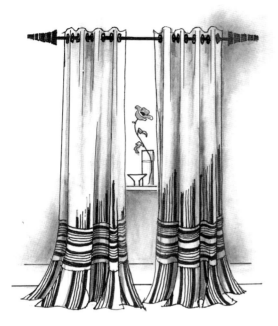

Stripes give a contemporary look to this design—
and using a broad band of the fabric horizontally
adds extra flair.

Create a tonal variation by using three different fabrics
in bands—place the darkest tone at the bottom.

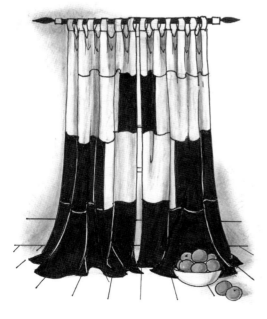

When using contrasting fabrics in squares, you can play
about with the layout of colors to create your own
geometric design.

On these giant stripe drapes the tabs are cut to the
width of the stripe for a co-ordinated look.

Modern

A single voile curtain with a braid machined on to create your own design. This is a great way to add something extra to a large picture window.

When you are using a wire tracking to hang your drapes, you must only use a lightweight fabric such as a voile.

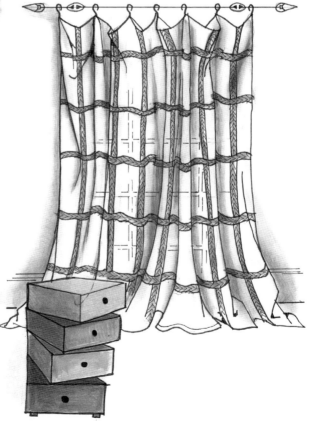

Here the shade is functional, but the fabric is just draped artistically over the pole.

A simple panel of fabric takes on a whole new style with the addition of deep fringing at the hem.

Modern

Traditional
and Modern
Designs

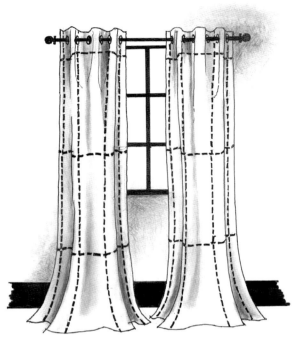

The leather thonging used to hang this drape is echoed by adding diagonal lines of leather thong lacing across the fabric.

A simple grid of saddle stitching in a contrast color on a plain drape.

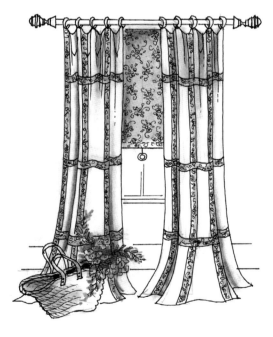

The fabric used to trim this drapery matches the floral roller shade behind and gives a homely country-style feel.

Different fabrics can be combined in one set of drapes—but make sure either the color or the design co-ordinates to hold the look together.

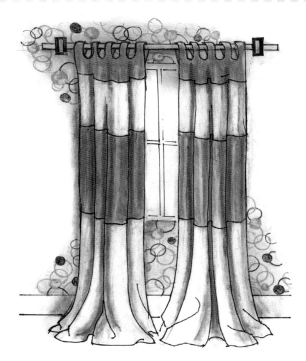

When making up drapes from blocks of fabric, you can alter the size of the blocks for extra interest.

Joining bands of contrast fabric means you can have the stripes any width that you choose.

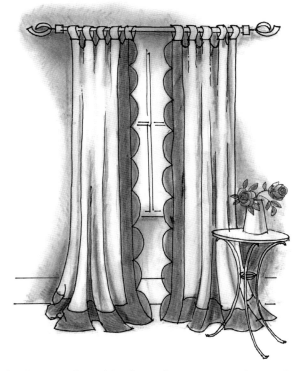

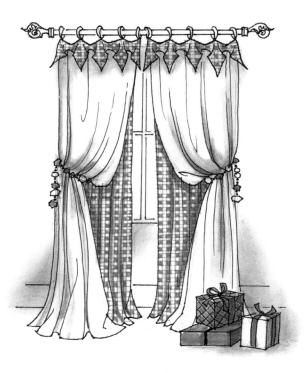

Adding a scalloped leading edge creates an interesting frame for the window.

A pointed turnover heading to match the functional drapes.

Modern

Traditional
and Modern
Designs

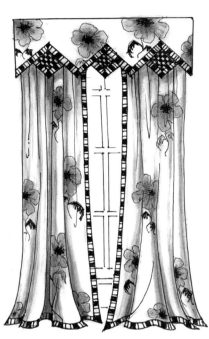

For an over-the-top design use big, bold fabrics combined with a co-ordinating stripe.

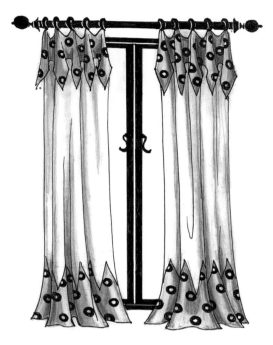

A handkerchief-point spotted contrast top is echoed in the matching band at the hem of these drapes.

Patchwork drapes are a great way to use up leftover pieces of fabric.

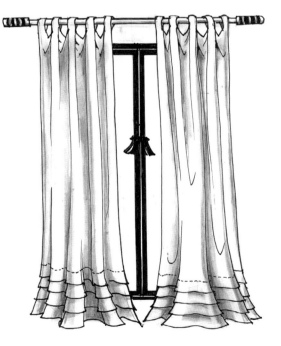

Wide tucks at the hem of these drapes add weight both visually and in reality, so they hang beautifully.

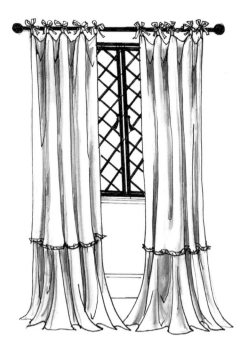

Delicate tie-headed drapes with deep ruffles on the hem.

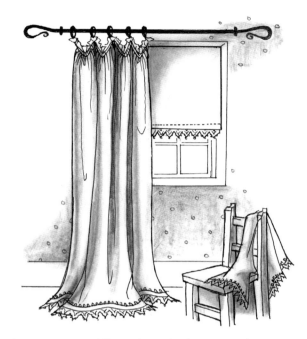

An unstructured linen drape is given extra interest with a crocheted lace hem, which is repeated along the base of the shade.

Short, striped drapes are fun and practical for a kitchen window.

A fun design using spots and stripes in matching colors.

Bay windows

These drapes are hung from a covered lathe—the center drapes pull both ways.

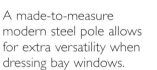

Traditional and Modern Designs

A made-to-measure modern steel pole allows for extra versatility when dressing bay windows.

These French windows in a deep recess have simple drapes on the outside of the recess, with a valance that runs right round the inside.

The curtain and valance on this bay recess are in a heavy dramatic fabric accentuated with deep bullion fringing.

Bay windows

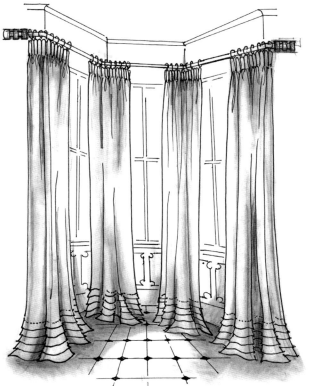

Small bays need simple drapes—
but the repeating bands of tucks at
the base add some extra interest
to this design.

When there are window seats, as
in this case, just have dress drapes
and functional shades.

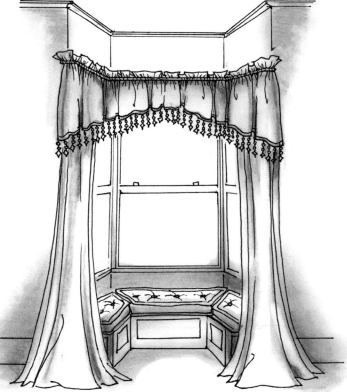

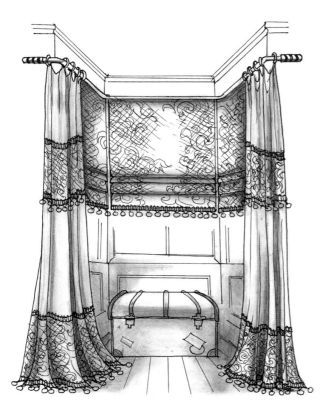

Shades can be designed to co-ordinate exactly with the drapes—here they are made in the same fabric as the decorative band on the drapes and have the same bobble fringe.

If there is seating under the window, shades on their own are often the best option.

Bay windows

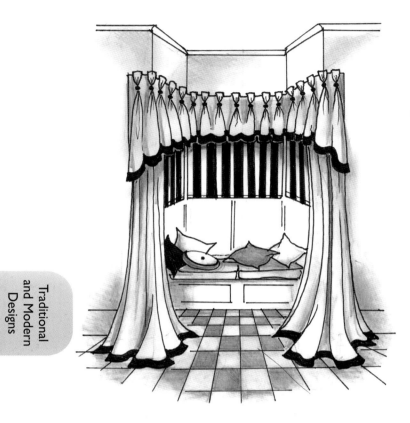

Dramatic striped shades are echoed in the contrast stripe on the dress drapes and valance.

Traditional and Modern Designs

Dress drapes with multi-colored rope tie-backs and a co-ordinating deep fringe on the valance. The colors of the rope are picked up in the stripes of the shades.

Another option for a bay window is to use two-tiered wooden shutters.

Roller shades look more finished with a pelmet or valance—here they are teamed with a quilted pelmet.

Italian stringing

Traditional and Modern Designs

Use the biggest print you can find for this design.

The spotted lining is visible when the drapes are pulled back.

A goblet pleat heading on Italian-strung drapes—but these should stay fixed, only the shade is used.

A simple drapery design with an elaborate carved pelmet.

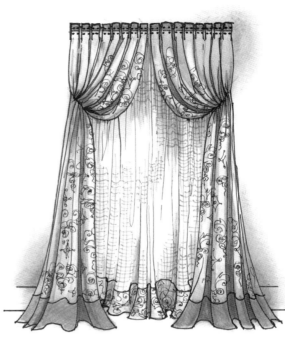

Italian-strung under-drapes teamed with softly folded dressed drapes.

Here the Italian-strung drapes are co-ordinated with the voile beneath by adding a wide band of drapery material as a border.

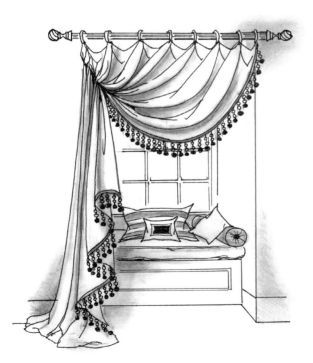

A cosy seating area is made more private with a simple Italian-strung drape.

Italian-strung dress drape with a scroll-printed roller shade.

Covered lathes

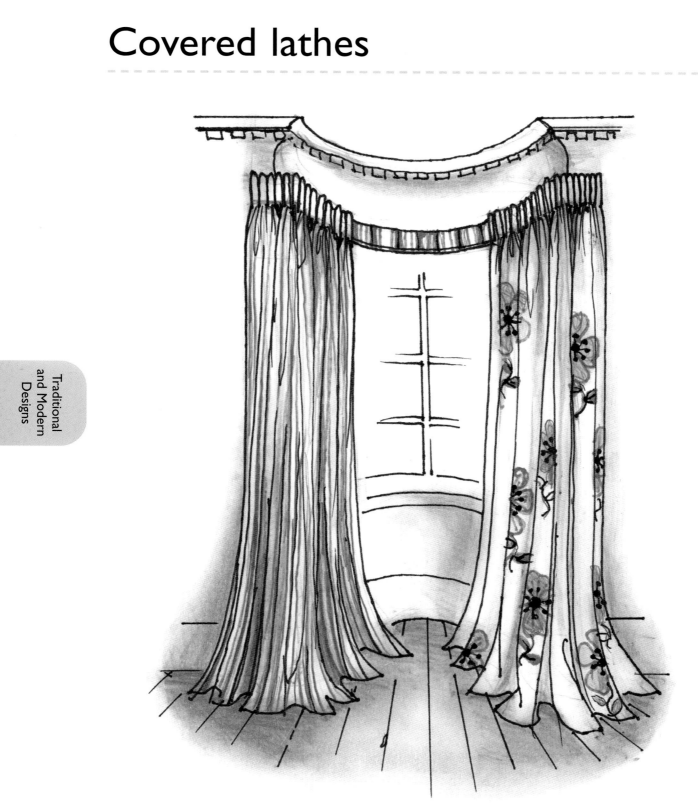

A covered lathe is essential for a window this
unusual shape.

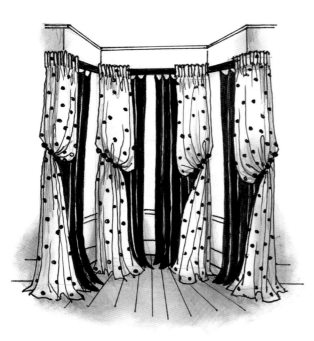

A covered lathe is very neat in a bay window.

One-sided drapes in black and white spotted silk, with a black covered lathe.

Here the striped contrast used on the leading edge matches the covered lathe.

Dress drapes

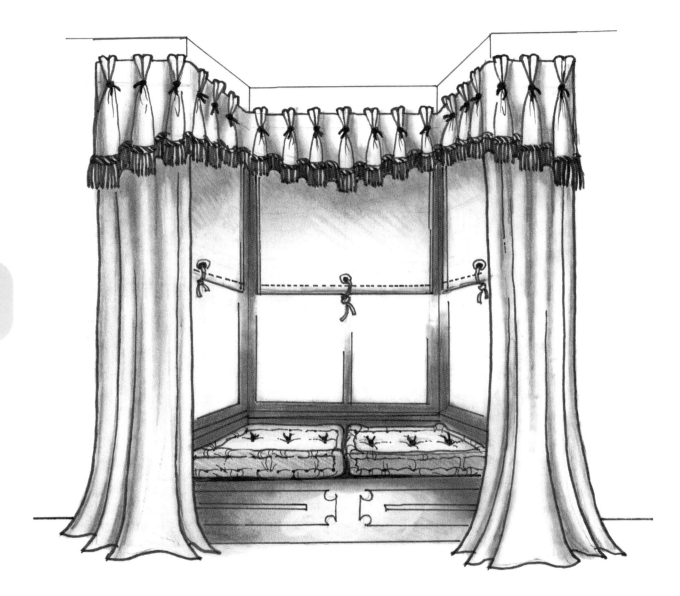

Traditional and Modern Designs

If there are objects in the way of the window, such as a window seat or heater, you can still have dress drapes—just add a functional shade underneath.

Dress drapes can be used in many ways—here are some more ideas for adding dress drapes over functional shades.

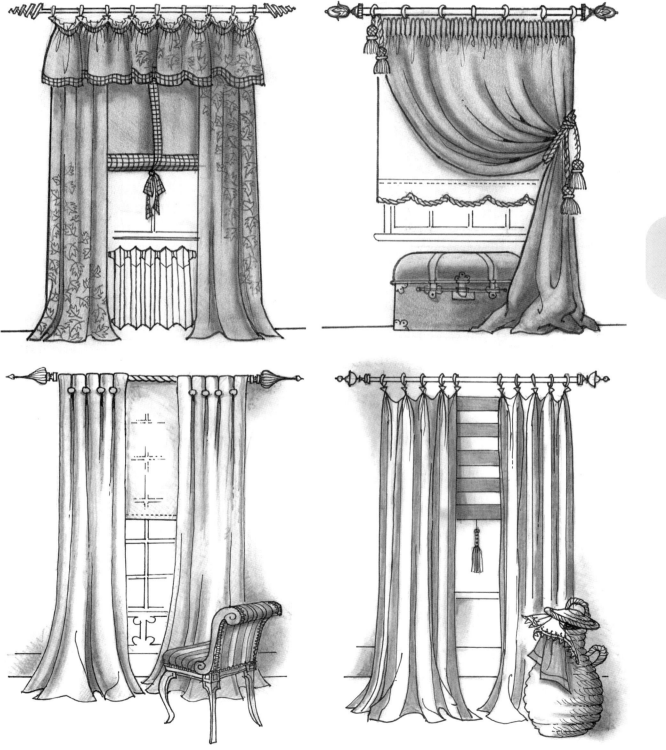

Voiles/sheers

Traditional
and Modern
Designs

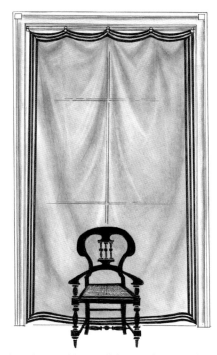

Ribbon borders add a stylish touch to a plain voile panel.

A beautiful lace panel needs no more than a simple pole to display it.

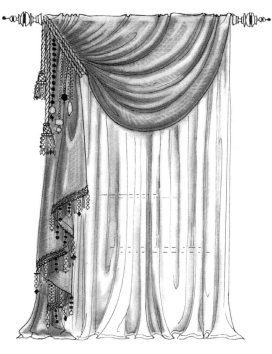

A draped, one-sided top drape with plenty of trim makes this voile design look stunning.

A one-sided top drape adds a touch of formality to this simple voile.

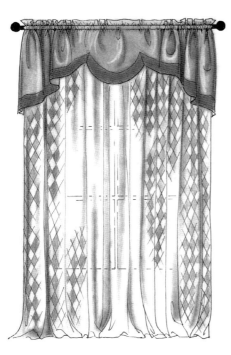

Patterned voile teamed with a toning valance on a rod pocket heading.

For a less formal look, hang the voiles on hooks and loops.

This valance is made from an old shawl, knotted to the pole.

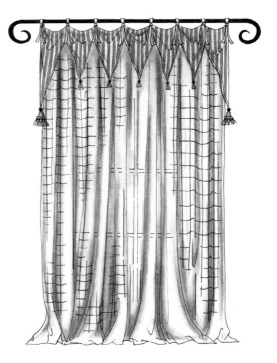

Points trimmed with tassels and gay stripes and checks are a fun look for a children's room.

Voiles/sheers

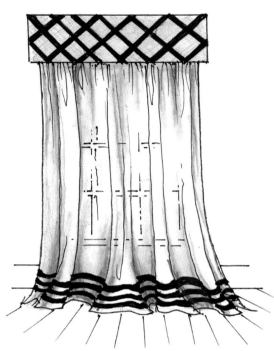

The wide braid used on the hem of these voiles is echoed in the lattice pattern on the pelmet.

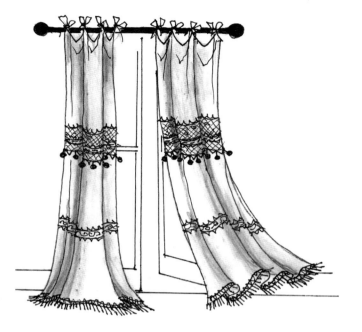

Add bands of different lace trim and a simple fringe on the hem.

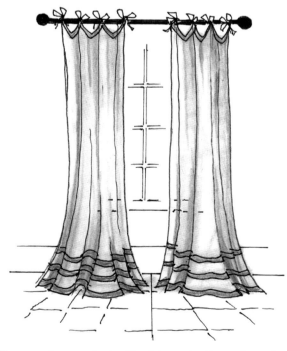

These voiles are tied with ribbons to the pole and matching ribbon is used to trim the hem.

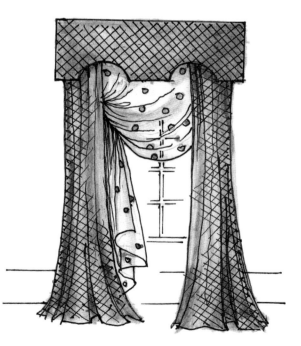

Spotted Italian-strung voile drapes under trellis fabric over-drapes.

A simple drapery design with added greenery for a garden room.

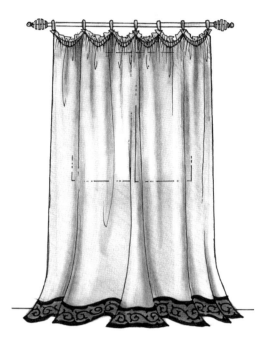

This plain drape is made special by using a wide jacquard ribbon on the hem.

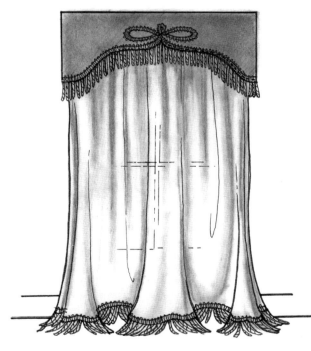

Gathered voile combined with a formal valance and co-ordinated with heavy fringing.

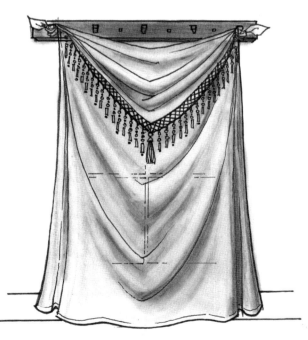

Plain voile panel with a heavy fringed shawl tied to the pole as a valance.

6

Alternatives to Drapes

Introduction to drapery alternatives...

There are alternatives...
Some people choose not to have drapes or shades to cover their windows. There is no real reason for them—although it is rather nice to close the drapes at night, rather like the end of a play, the day is over. It is cosier too and does help to make the room feel warmer. In the age of double glazing, perhaps it is just a habit, but some windows look unfinished without something to dress them up.

Some people can't sleep if there is a flicker of light in the room—in which case light resistant shades behind the drapes are the answer. Kitchens and bathrooms look great with wooden shutters, and a wonderful old screen would give privacy but allow lots of light to stream in above. Here are a few window coverings that might look good in your home and are easy to make as well.

Panels

Panels are so versatile. They not only look good but also provide a cheaper alternative to drapery since they use less fabric. The panels hang from tracking fixed on the ceiling and can be operated electronically. Although the cost of the ceiling tracking is high, eventually some manufacturer will produce a cheaper version. Panels are used in many offices where the windows are large. It is best if there is enough "stack back" either side of the window, so that when the panels are open they can be stored at the side to allow plenty of light into the room. There are several panel designs on the next few pages and you will see that there are various permutations: either with one big panel if the window is not too wide, or in sets of two or three.

Dormer windows

The two problems with dormer windows is that they are often quite small and the top of the window or the ceiling above is a strange shape – either sloping or pointed. Since you will want to leave as much of the window clear as possible to let in light, and the top of any treatment has to be fixed, the options become somewhat limited. However, there are some things you can do that will look very acceptable – see pages 162–3 for some possible solutions to the problem.

Café and short curtains

Café curtains are generally are made with a rod pocket heading and hung on a rod about halfway up the window. They are used mainly to give a little privacy—they were invented to screen diners sitting in the window from people passing on the sidewalk, while still allowing them to look out. They are useful in a domestic situation for a similar reason, perhaps if the front of a house is right on the sidewalk so people can look in as they walk past. Old-fashioned cafés often use them in lace or gingham to create an old-world atmosphere. In America they seem to be particularly popular.

In general, I am not a fan of short drapery, but sometimes it is the best option—on a door for instance, or for a cottage interior.

Difficult windows

It is often best just to leave difficult windows alone if they are very odd shapes—it can look very silly to try to cover a strange shape with a piece of fabric and hope that it works. So unless the window has to have drapes for some important reason—privacy or to screen daylight—just leave it without any window dressing at all. However, if you must have something, there are a few ideas shown on pages 164–71 that may help to solve your problem window.

Window dressing

Dressing a window using unusual items can be great fun and there are hundreds of ways to do it. Some windows benefit from a little bit of dressing up—just putting some simple muslin up at the glass will defuse the light coming into the room. Other decorative ideas include stained glass, colored marbles, pebbles and strips of colored ribbon.

Remember, it is not necessary to cover every part of a window, especially if there is a spectacular view—why would you want to block out a great view with drapes?

Portières

Portières are generally one-sided drapes, which act as a "door" in a corridor—hence the name. They are pulled back to one side with a tie-back or hold-back, or may be Italian-strung. If the drape needs to be closed on occasion, the first option is better.

The term portière can also be used to describe window or door coverings with a rod pocket heading top and bottom, in which the fabric is slotted onto rods attached at one side of the window only. The portière can then swing open and closed as required, for access to the window.

Panels

A sliding panel is an ideal solution to achieve some privacy.

For a wide window, three or more panels can stack and slide.

Braid and deep bullion fringe are repeated in the other soft furnishings nearby for a co-ordinated look.

Panels don't have to be plain—use large, important trims down the leading edge.

Panels

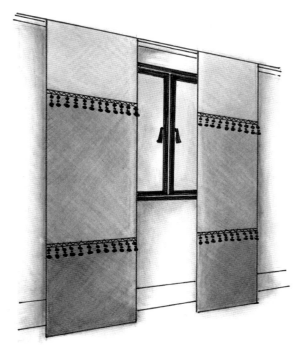

Simple trims add some extra style.

Ribbons and braids can be combined for a unique look.

A chevron border looks simple and modern.

The curves in the paisley print fabric band are echoed in the scalloped edge at the top of this panel.

Bold checks look best on a large picture window in a modern setting.

A single panel has a design of appliquéd squares and a matching border.

Panels

Panels that don't match create a sense of fun and frivolity.

Mondrian style for a set of French windows.

Large bold stripes are very effective on a single panel.

Huge chevrons need a modern bold interior, such as a loft apartment.

Eyelet holes and string lacing give a nautical look.

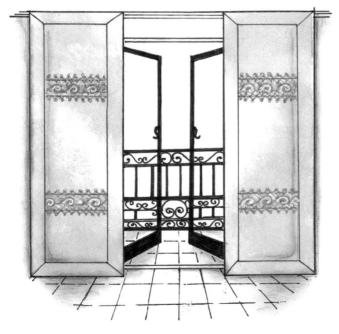

Lace inset bands create a softer, more romantic feeling.

Panels

A single panel shows off the design of this beautiful lace.

A translucent panel with scattered appliqué leaves gives privacy without losing too much light.

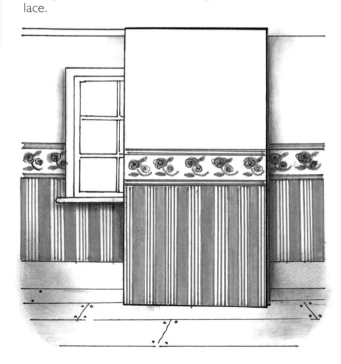

Covering the window panel with wallpaper to match the walls will create a streamlined feel for a simple interior.

Panels are great for a boy's room—a wipe-clean surface will allow them to express their creativity!

Using sliding panels across an alcove is a cheaper option than having a closet made—and you can ring the changes by replacing the fabric with a different print.

Sliding panels are fun and practical to hide the clutter in a child's room.

Short/café curtains

Café curtains are ideal for a window next to a door to add a touch of privacy.

Rod pocket headings are best for café curtains that normally will not be drawn aside.

Hooks and loops are another option for a fixed café curtain.

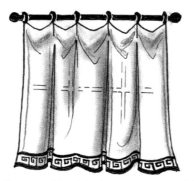

Inverted pleats and braid trim create a stylish feel.

Knotting a scarf or fabric panel onto the pole is a neat option.

An unstructured heading and pulled back corner revealing a contrast lining gives a much softer look.

A gingham border and ties are ideal for a cottage interior.

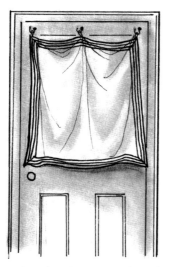

A fabric panel on hooks over a glass door panel gives privacy.

For a more dressy option, use a miniature drape complete with tab heading and tucked hem.

Dormer windows

Roman shade shaped into the point of the ceiling above the dormer.

A shade is the best option for a window covering in a confined space.

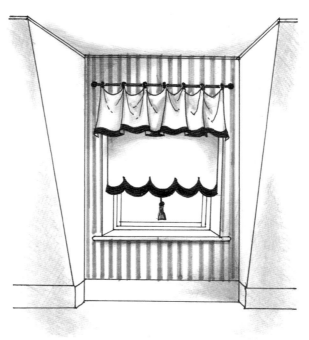

When adding a valance to a shade, make sure it sits high enough so it does not block out too much light.

The translucent panel in the center of this London shade lets in extra light.

Here, the fabric panel trimmed with bobbles is just for fun, and the drape is functional.

Matching windows look good with matching Oriental shades.

Difficult windows

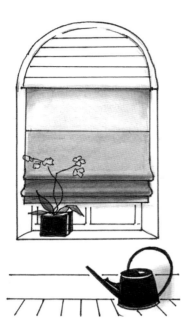

A fixed pleated pelmet over a Roman shade.

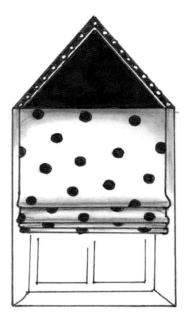

This Roman shade has a shaped top which is held in place with studs. The Roman shade is attached.

Roman shades are an ideal solution with an unusually shaped window.

A long, thin window looks stylish with a lambrequin teamed with a shaped roller shade and pull tassel.

Sandblasted glass is a good solution for a bathroom, offering privacy but maximum natural light.

164

When fitting a shade into an unusual shape, make an accurate template in paper first.

The scalloped curves of this Austrian shade echo the curved center of the window shape.

With roller shades, anything is possible!

A stepped pelmet follows the shape of the stairs beneath.

Difficult windows

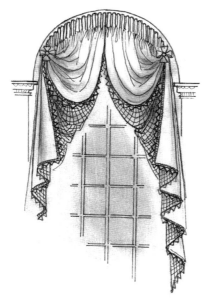

Swags and tails on a formal arched window.

An exotic stencil does away with the need for any other window dressing.

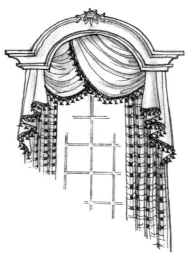

A shaped pelmet teamed with swags and tails for a really formal look.

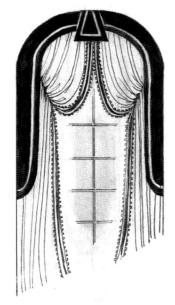

Try teaming a lambrequin with lightweight Italian-strung drapery.

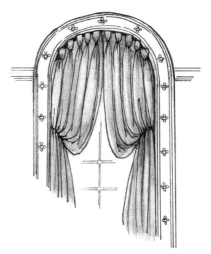

A decorative border and Italian-strung drapery with goblet heading.

Alternatives to Curtains

Folding shutters are a good option if drapes are not suitable.

Double folding shutters on a small, wide window over a radiator.

Free-standing four-panel screen used instead of drapes or shades.

A four-panel screen can be a temporary or a permanent solution.

Alternatives/other options

Display pebbles, shells or glass balls on the cross bars of a multi-paned window.

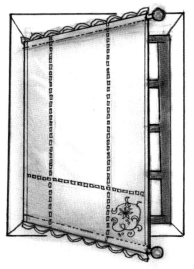

A linen portière opens out easily when necessary, but holds a panel of fabric taut over the window.

Stained glass is a long-term solution for a hard-to-get-at window.

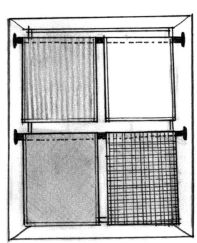

Hanging panels on a tension rod— ring the changes by switching the panels around.

Lengths of beaded ribbon in differing designs and colors for a fun look.

A simple fabric panel folded up and held with ribbon ties is quick and easy to make.

For an instant solution, knot an old shawl to the pole.

Seasonal foliage brings a natural look into the interior.

A bagged-out swag and tail draped over the pole.

Traditional portières

A lovely carved wooden pelmet is combined with an exciting mix of spots and flowers in this double portière drapery.

Use a big tassel fringe on this Italian-strung portière drapery.

For a true over-the-top-look, use as
many strings of beads as possible.

A heavy, thick tweed portière with
deep wool fringing—in case you
live in a castle!

Modern portières

These voile half-panels give some privacy, but still allow lots of light into the area.

A pretty, dotted Swiss voile portière dresses the window, but is easy to open when necessary.

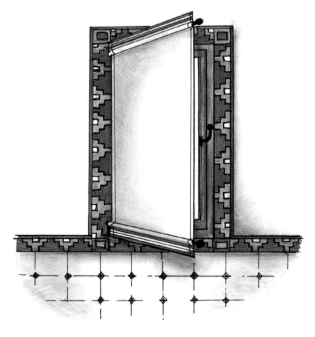

Portières are ideal for a bathroom, allowing the window to be opened for ventilation.

A simple linen portière with embossed initials for a personal touch.

An opening panel allows a wonderful view to be admired when privacy is not needed.

Translucent portières have a distinctly Japanese flavor.

Obscuring glass panels in the door can be difficult—a portière is one possible solution.

173

Dressing a window

This pretty translucent fabric has a lovely trim weighted with drop crystals.

A fretwork pelmet gives a simple and stylish look all on its own.

This half shade edged with chevrons is ideal for the kitchen.

Dress shade with a chevron-pointed hem trimmed with lace and tassels.

Sometimes drapes are not required at all for a great look.

Wonderful strings of crystals, hung in a carefully graded diagonal.

A pretty valance trimmed with a wide band of lace is all this window needs.

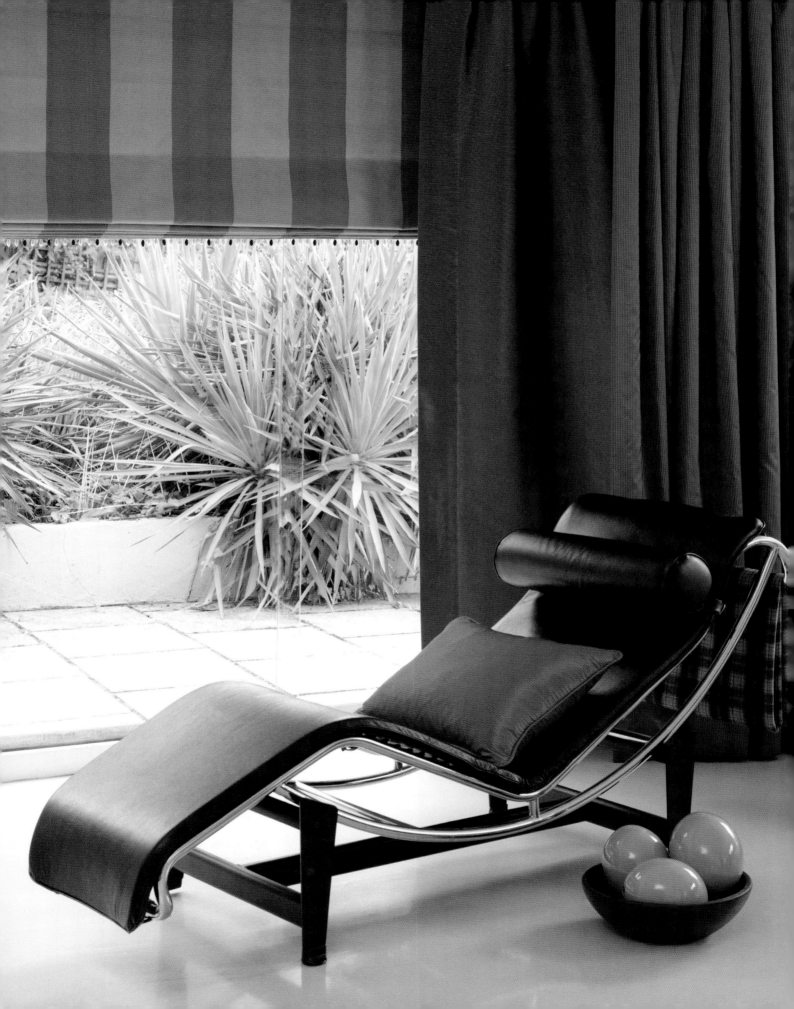

7

Shades and Blinds

Introduction to shades...

A few words of advice...
There are a few instances where shades don't work—
if the windows are not suitable for shades for some
reason then more than likely they will not be right for
drapes either. So I would generally just dress the
window so that it doesn't look bare, and move on!

Roman shades

This type of shade is a softer version of the roller shade; it
hangs flat when it is in the down position and folds neatly up
into horizontal pleats when it is in the up position. The shade is
fixed to a covered batten with the aid of "touch and close" tape
(known in the UK as Velcro®) and operated by lift cords which
pass through the china barrels secured by brass, chrome or
wooden cleats. You can have a right or left side operation.

   Roman shades tend to be the most popular type of shade,
mainly because they are uncluttered and therefore suit most
room schemes. They are often lined and even interlined
depending upon the type of fabric being used. Use them
unlined in place of the old-fashioned voiles used for privacy.

Austrian shades

If like me you don't particularly like these shades you will still
find some clients insisting on them. They are very fussy but do
fit into a formal setting very well. I use them sometimes with
simple dressed drapes or a panel and that looks quite good. You
will find a few examples throughout the book.

Linen fold

These shades are completely unstructured and I like the way
they fit so well into a contemporary setting. There are no poles
or rods and, unlike Roman shades, they are not "trained" and
therefore fall in a relaxed style. As the center fabric is often
voile or an open weave, avoid having any seams across the
fabric or this can look a mess. So the maximum width of your
shade will be the width of your fabric, which is generally about
72in (180cm) but there is no restriction on length. The borders
have to be a more solid fabric, such as linen, as there are eyelet
holes down the side for the cords to run through, which when
pulled makes the shade go up into folds.

Cascades

These are quite formal and are similar to Romans but when
they are in the down position they stay in their folds. A Cascade
is handmade and attached to a covered batten and, like the
Roman shade, it is operated by the same cording system. The
pleats retain their shape by the steel rods inserted into the
horizontal pockets at the back of the blind. Avoid using cascades
in bay windows, as they tend to be a bit bulky.

Oriental shades

Very basic shades and easy to make. They simply roll up and down by cords that pass through rings; the cords can be in contrast colours or matched to the top fabric. Normally the Oriental shade is "bagged" out—this means that there are two fabrics, one for the front and one for the contrast at the back, machined together on the wrong side and then turned inside out—therefore, the quantities of fabric are equal. It is a good idea to add a machine hem stitch to the edge of the two fabrics because if the fabric is too thick the blind will not roll up and down smoothly. If you are having them unlined you must have French seams, as the seams will show when rolled and will look unsightly from the outside when in the down position.

London shades

These are quite formal shades and are best used in a formal setting. The shades should be lined and interlined (not too heavy) with a contrast color fabric for the inverted pleats. Used mainly to dress a window, for instance in a hall or on a landing, but be careful as this shade has to be well made and positioned properly or it can look disastrous. They are very useful for arched windows, as the top of the shade can be shaped to fit almost any shape of window—but you will obviously need to give the manufacturer a template to follow.

Shutters

These are my favorite type of shade. They are the most versatile of all window coverings. They are not cheap, but I think they are worth every penny you spend on them. Make sure you go to a good manufacturer, as there are many cheap copies and they will always cause problems. They are permanently fixed to the windows and can be hinged back completely or left in situ and the louvers moved to the open or closed position manually. By moving the louvers to the open position you can fine tune the amount of light you want in the room. Shutters can be spray painted any color or you can have them made in various types of wood such as mahogany, beech, pine, cherry or oak. The louvers come in several sizes the most popular are $1\frac{7}{8}$in (4.8cm), $2\frac{1}{2}$in (6.4cm) or $3\frac{1}{2}$in (8.9cm) but each manufacturer has their own specific sizes. Always make sure that the middle rails match your window frame. Shutters work really well in bay windows and can be custom made to any shape of window. They are especially good in conservatories, for Velux® windows and can also be used as closet doors. I buy my shutters for my clients from a particular manufacturer who plants a tree for every order for shutters—nice thought!

Shades and Blinds

Basic shades

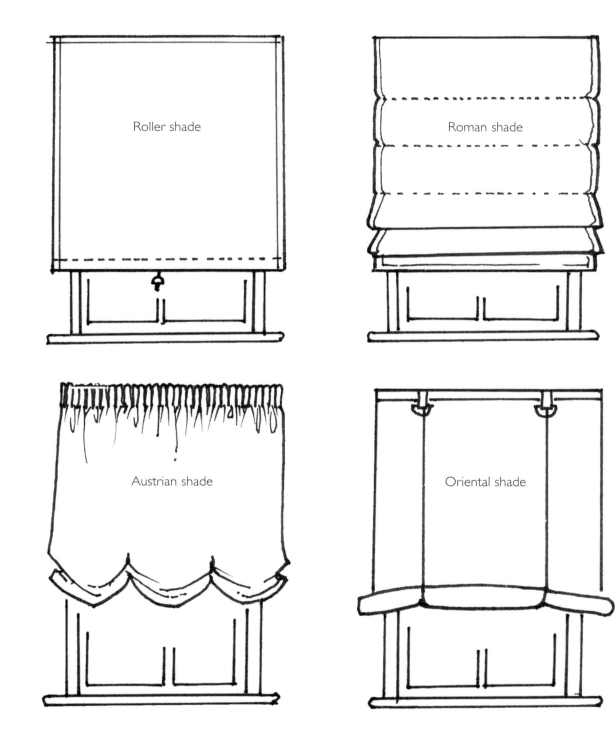

Roller shade

Roman shade

Austrian shade

Oriental shade

Linen fold

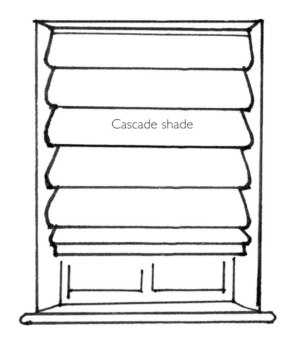

Cascade shade

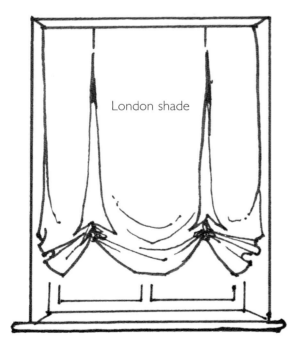

London shade

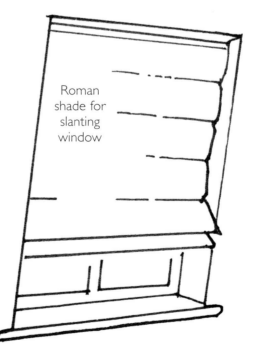

Roman shade for slanting window

Basic roller shades

These were the first shades on the market and during the last few years have gone out of fashion, but they seem to be coming back in a big way now. They are very versatile, suitable for most windows, and can be dressed up in many ways to suit different situations.

If you use a translucent fabric, these roller shades can replace those old-fashioned-looking netting curtains, letting in natural light but still giving a certain amount of privacy.

If you are thinking of having light-resistant lining in your bedroom drapes to stop the light coming in, then use light-resistant roller shades in the windows instead and cover them with flimsy drapes to soften the look—it works much better.

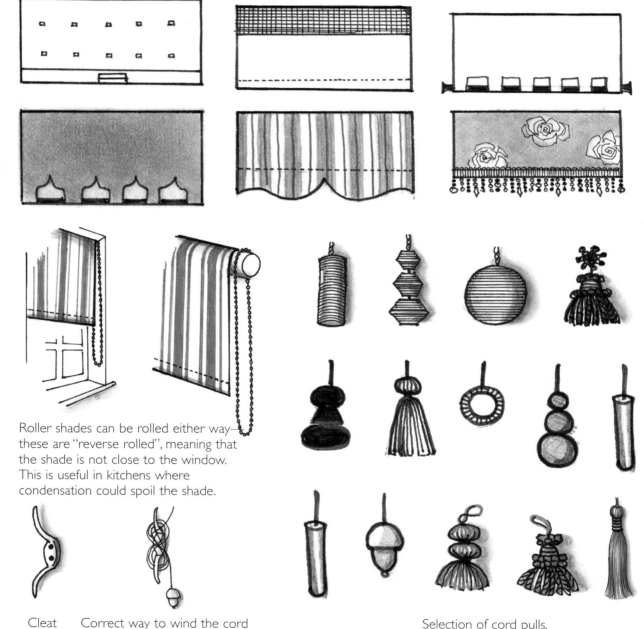

Roller shades can be rolled either way—these are "reverse rolled", meaning that the shade is not close to the window. This is useful in kitchens where condensation could spoil the shade.

Cleat   Correct way to wind the cord when shade is in the "up'" position.

Selection of cord pulls.

Curtains with blinds

Pretty sheer drapes dress the window, but the scalloped shade behind cuts out light and provides full privacy.

Shade trimmed with crystal fringe to match the drape.

Lovely unstructured drape pulled to one side and tied with a big satin bow, over a crenellated shade with a pull bar.

Roller shades

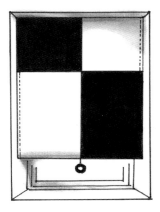

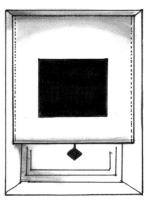

Combining fabrics offers many variations, such as this checkerboard...

... or this inset square.

Roller shades don't have to have a pull cord—this one has a metal pull bar.

A simple roller shade can look stunning in the right fabric.

Try combining the shade with a lambrequin.

A fretwork pelmet looks very stylish.

Roller shades are ideal in the kitchen—try using a co-ordinating border.

Using insets and braids means you can create your own unique design.

A translucent roller shade will let in some light.

Lambrequins

Simple curved lambrequin in striped fabric.

Shaping the arch adds an extra decorative element to this scroll fabric lambrequin.

Any shape can be made... this one adds a curve that contrasts with the plaid fabric.

Diagonal stripes on this pointed arch lambrequin.

Shades and Blinds

Fretwork lambrequins

Points and curves work well together.

Carved and scrollwork lambrequin in wood.

Roman shades

Simple stripes for a minimalist interior.

Lush brocade fabric for the period look.

Stripes and a bold border work in this country interior.

Japanese cherry blossom adds an Oriental look to this kitchen.

Roman shades

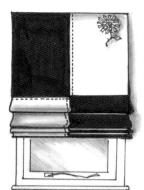

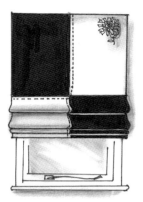

Bold brickwork-design in Russian braid gives a sharp modern look.

Matching checkerboard shades look smart on a double window.

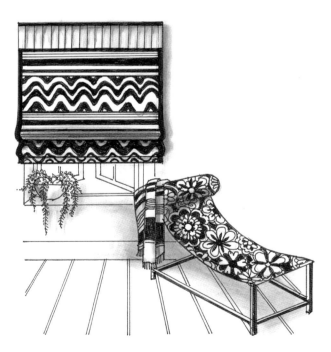

A bold geometric print makes this Roman shade a major feature of the room.

Pretty lace Roman shades are ideal to soften this modern bathroom.

With valances

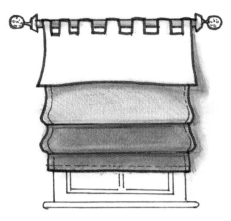

Roman shade with plain tab valance.

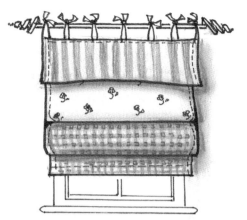

Multi-fabric Roman shade with tied valance for a
pretty, informal look.

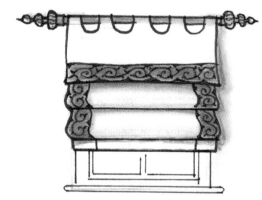

Scalloped valance trimmed with a matching border.

Soft tucked valance on rings, trimmed with a lace
border.

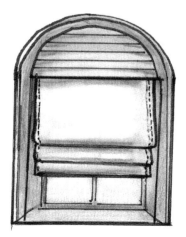

Tucked valance over saddle-stitched Roman shade.

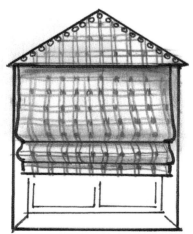

Shaped valance to fit into a pointed window.

With valances

The layered look—bands of different fabric on the shade topped with another for the valance.

This shade is edged with a wide jacquard ribbon, as is the matching valance.

Masculine plaids are softened with this gathered valance.

Austrian shades

Giant polka dots and gingham trim look great on gathered fabric.

Sheer Austrian shade with fretwork pelmet.

The pretty rose print on this shade matches the carved roses on the pelmet.

Bold stripes and a Greek key pelmet for the Empire look.

Matching fabric for shades, stool and table cloth for a co-ordinated look.

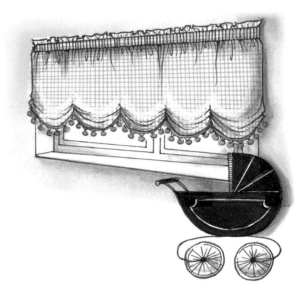

Simple gingham with a bobble fringe is great for a nursery.

A richly patterned fabric gives a lush feel to this shaped shade.

Sheer lace makes a great shade that will let light into the room even when down.

Austrian shades

Shades and
Blinds

A beautiful silk shade with heavy crystal trim.

A slotted heading on a voile shade with contrast ruffles.

Traditional-looking design with plenty of ropes and tassels.

Translucent fabric lets in light, but the pencil pleat heading adds a touch of formality.

With drapes or panels

A dress drape and co-ordinating shade.

Bright plaids for shade and drape give a cheerful Scottish look.

Sliding panels in a range of fabrics—the curves of the matching shade soften the geometric effect.

Giant prints look good on panels, but would be lost on the gathered fabric of a shade.

Linen folds

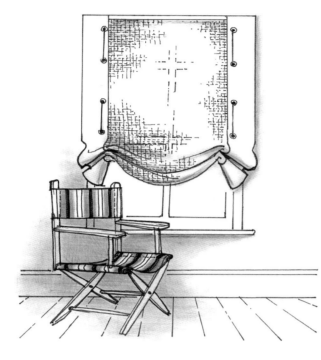

Sailcloth, eyelets and rope for a touch of the seaside...

... and teamed with gingham for a country feel.

A valance with a rod pocket heading and bobble fringe teamed with a simple linen fold shade.

Linen folds are great for a country interior.

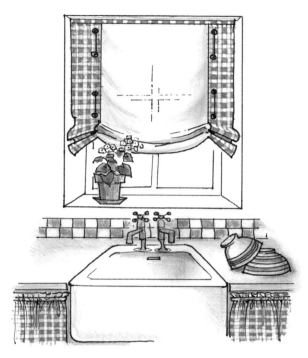

Checked border to match the tiled frieze in this kitchen.

In this modern, minimalist bathroom drapes would be too fussy.

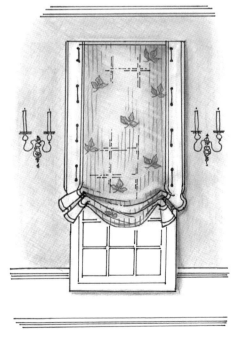

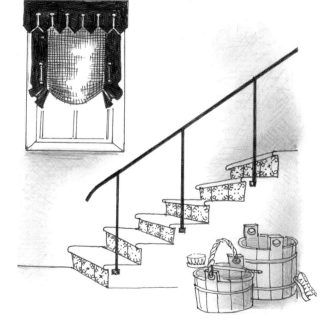

Lights on either side of this window leave no room for drapes.

Windows on stairs always look better with a shade rather than drapes.

Cascades

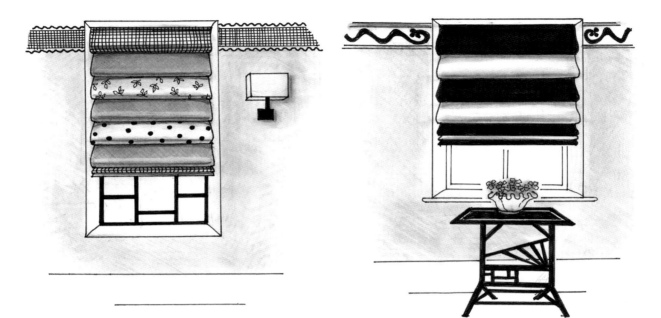

Using different fabrics adds variety and interest and creates an informal look. Here, the top panel matches the wall frieze.

Stripes of bold color co-ordinate with the wall frieze—make sure the width of the top panel lines up with the edges of the frieze.

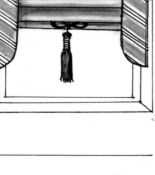

This shaped lambrequin gives an Eastern feel to the design.

Using a simple curved lambrequin and Russian braid gives a more military look.

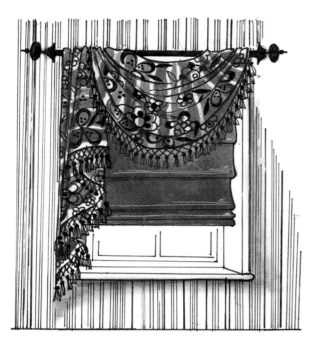

A shawl draped over the pole softens the angular feel of a shade.

Draped fabric creates an informal swag and tails.

A fretwork pelmet conceals and finishes off the top of a cascade shade.

Here, the ironwork pelmet has a matching design at the sill.

Cascades

Cascade shades look good in a recessed window.

Add a rod pocket valance trimmed with tassel fringe for a more luxurious look.

A formal setting demands a more formal treatment—such as this complex double valance trimmed with rope.

A heavy fabric pelmet and valance, trimmed with matching rope and bullion fringe, add gravitas to this design.

Stunning fabric combined with a triangular point hem embellished with tassels.

A stenciled pelmet is a great option for a child's room. Two smaller matching shades are a better option in this situation than one large one.

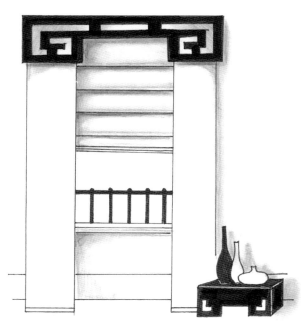

Create a calm, Oriental feel with this shaped pelmet combined with cascade and panels.

Panels combined with shades are a less fussy option than drapes.

Oriental shades

Oriental shades are the easiest type to make. Line the panel with a contrast fabric for a great effect.

Florals combined with gingham are a soft and pretty option.

A dramatic chevron design is backed with a plain, strong color.

An Oriental shade is ideal to control the light in a work area.

Translucent Oriental shades provide privacy without cutting down on natural light.

Matching windows with matching plain Oriental shades are very effective.

A fretwork pelmet and a contrast-lined over-drape make this simple shade look more dressy.

Japanese sliding paper panels and cherry blossom printed on the shade for a truly Oriental look.

London shades

The boldly printed floral fabric is displayed to advantage on this London shade, which is teamed with a pencil-pleated valance.

A strongly contrasting border accentuates the shape of this shade and its valance.

Shades are an ideal option for arched windows...

... of all types. Here, the braided trim highlights the curve of the window shape.

Shades and
Blinds

A traditional London shade with rope trim to the pelmet and matching tasseled fringe.

An unusual chevron pelmet echoes the chevron design of the dado frieze.

A plain design, but the strips of ribbon and bows on the pelmet add a charming touch.

The inverted pleats on valance and shade are lined with a contrasting fabric.

Shutters

Shutters are a great option for French windows—make sure they open the opposite way to the doors.

Whatever the window shape, a shutter can be made to fit.

Two-tier shutters allow the option of having one or the other level open for more light while still giving a certain amount of privacy.

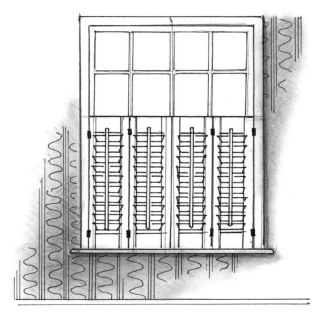

Half shutters offer privacy but maximum natural light.

Angular shapes are quite possible with shutters.

With sloping ceilings, the shutter can be fixed but with movable slats to control the light.

Extra-wide slats look stylish in a modern bathroom.

A fixed shutter panel in the arch, with opening shutters for the window beneath—a very classical look.

Wooden and metal Venetians

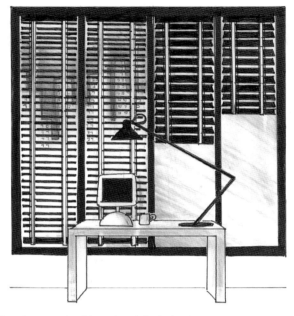

Simple wooden Venetian blinds look stunning in black.

Triple window with three matching wooden Venetian blinds.

Shades and Blinds

Metal Venetian blinds look simple and stylish in a modern interior.

Venetian blinds are ideal for those odd situations where other treatments won't work.

The webbing on Venetian blinds can be a matching or a contrasting color.

Try painting the slats to match the colors in the interior.

Velux® blinds

Rooflights such as Velux® windows need blinds specially made with the correct fixings.

Another Velux® blind—ideal in bathrooms.

8

Beds

Introduction to beds...

A few words of advice...
Your bed is the most important piece of furniture in your home. Don't try to economize in any way. Buy your bed from a good department store with a proper bed department where the staff are trained to advise you. Buy a good make like Hypnos, Staples, Vi-Spring or Reylon. These manufacturers know about beds, as they have been in the business for a long time.

Bedcovers

These are not as popular as they used to be, as most people now prefer to have a duvet. There are such pretty duvet covers that there is no need to have a bedcover as well. On page 216, I have just shown one shape and some variations for if you prefer a bedcover. On page 217, I have given you some ideas for designs with valances.

Headboards

Fabric headboards can be made in many, many different shapes. Every now and again the fashion changes and so do the headboards! Most of my clients at the moment like to have very tall ones; I am not sure why this is but, as I say, it's the fashion.

Iron headboards look nice although they can be uncomfortable—but I suppose you have to have a little discomfort if you want to get the right look!

Wooden headboards can be homemade to give a rustic feel to the bedroom or they can be sophisticated carved Louis XIV copies. Modern wooden beds often have the headboard incorporated into the frame and the mattress is laid on top of wooden slats—very uncomfortable!

Coronas

These are like a coronet over the bed and generally have a valance edged with some kind of trim. Then a pair of dress drapes come from under the corona and they are caught over a hold-back or hook on either side of the headboard.

Canopies

A canopy is a piece of fabric draped over a bed purely for effect. If you are fixing it to the ceiling, be sure you find a secure fixing to take the weight.

Half tester and four-poster

A half tester is like a corona, but it goes the whole width of the bed. Drapes are fixed from the half tester and they fall neatly behind the headboard.

Four-poster beds nearly always have drapes around them. This originated from the need to keep warm or for privacy. With a traditional four-poster there is often a very elaborate silk dressing above the bed with pin tucks and pleats. This is a good opportunity to use trim on the edge of the valance and the drapes are held back to the four posts with tassel tie-backs. Modern four-posters are made in wood, steel or in fact anything goes. The drapes are not so formal and are sometimes casually just thrown over the frame.

Children's bedrooms

Bedrooms for children need to have plenty of storage boxes and book shelves. A nice idea is to incorporate a workstation into the room somehow. Little girls' rooms need more hanging space and boys need shelving for their football gear. It is fun to give the room a theme that can be changed as the child grows up.

Buying a bed

Dos

1 Lie on the bed in the shop, properly, with your eyes shut, and really think about the comfort. Nobody will laugh at you, and if they do so what! You are going to sleep on this bed half your life so get it right.

2 Buy a summer duvet with 4.5 tog upwards and a winter one with 10.5 tog upwards. Remember to have your duvets cleaned regularly and hang them on the clothes line to air once a month.

3 Choose your pillows carefully. I never bothered with anything special, a pillow is a pillow I thought, but a friend told me about her goose down pillow and how well she slept and I thought I would go into my local store and buy one for myself as an experiment. Well, I have never looked back. I can't believe that most of my long life I have been sleeping on rubbish pillows when all the time there was a goose down pillow waiting to whisk me off to dreamland!

4 Buy a topper to go on top of your mattress, however good your mattress is you still should go for a topper. A topper is simply a mattress cover; it is generally quilted and stuffed with down. It feels as if you are lying on a feather bed, which is divine but real feather beds are not very good for your back.

5 Have a cashmere or knit blanket at the bottom of the bed for those chilly nights—it's lovely to cuddle up to in the middle of the night!

6 Have a padded headboard for comfort—wooden and iron ones look great, but they are not for sitting in bed reading the Sunday papers!

7 Spend just a little extra and buy Egyptian cotton sheets or duvet covers. I know they need ironing but the difference in feel is worth it.

Don'ts

1 Don't buy a bed with storage under the mattress, as then the base is hard with no springs, so no matter how much you spend on a mattress the bed is always going to be hard.

2 Don't pay extra for an orthopedic bed just because you think it is the smart thing to do. If you have a bad back you may need one for medical reasons, but generally people just feel it guarantees a good bed. But why pay double the price for an orthopedic label when most manufacturers have a type of orthopedic mattress in their range at half the price?

3 Valances to match "non iron" sheets. Have one made just to cover the bed base in the same fabric as your curtains or bedspread—it looks much better and is worth the extra money.

4 Don't have your bed with its back to the light. Try to arrange the room so you can look out of the window as it can be quite depressing with the light behind you and if you are lucky enough to have a view you won't be able to see it!

5 Black satin sheets—that look is over and have you ever tried to iron them?

6 Avoid very heavy blankets on the bed; it is better to have a duvet or sheets with soft knit blankets. Heavy blankets can make you feel quite claustrophobic in the night.

Headboards

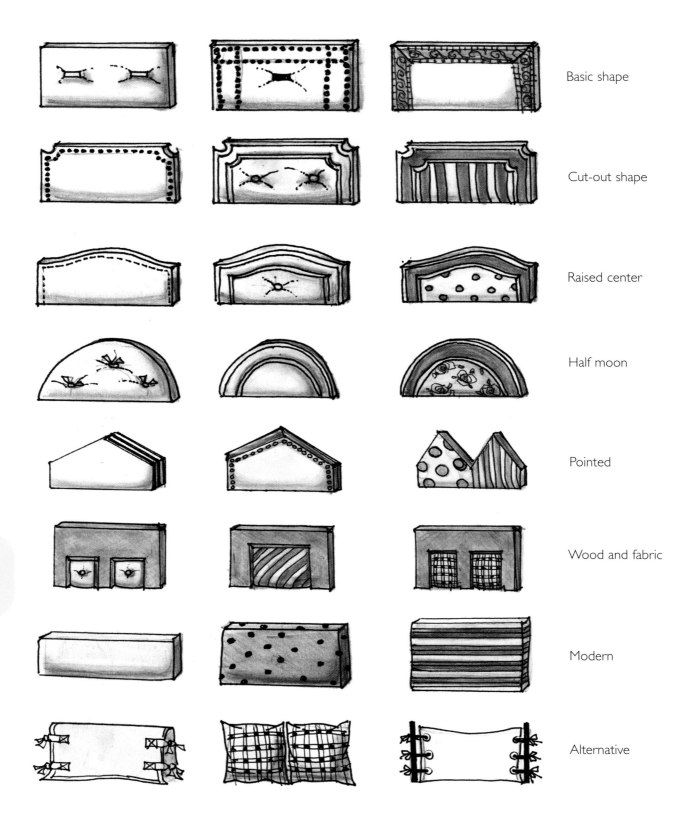

Basic shape

Cut-out shape

Raised center

Half moon

Pointed

Wood and fabric

Modern

Alternative

Beds

Bedcovers

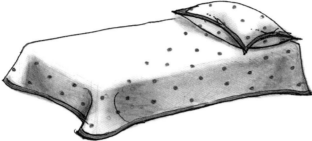

A basic throwover bedspread.

Bedcovers are ideal for bold prints, as the large area means they are displayed to advantage.

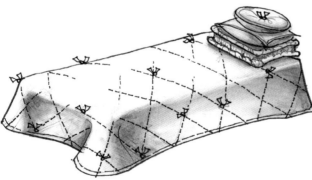

A quilted cover decorated with American knots.

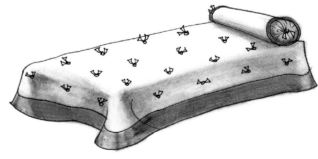

Knotted ties made from the same fabric as the border.

Valances

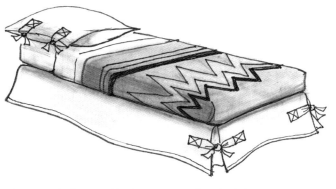

Inverted pleats with ties—carry the tied theme onto the pillow too.

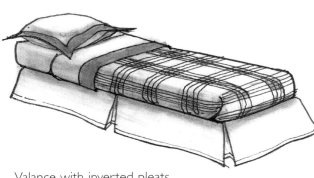

Valance with inverted pleats.

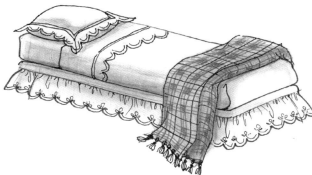

Pretty gathered and scalloped edge valance.

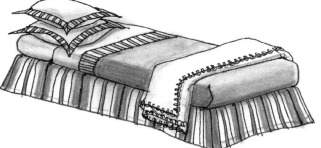

Simple striped box valance.

Padded headboards

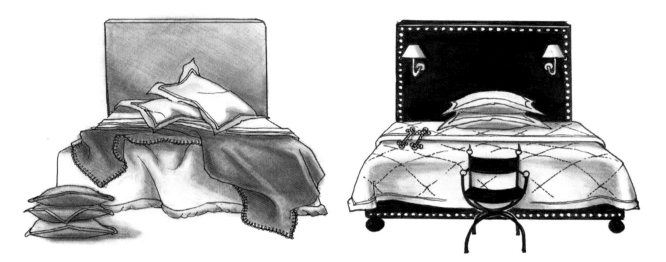

A tall padded headboard.

Studded headboard with lights and base to match.

A low, thick headboard with a screen behind to complete the look.

A fun bed using lots of colorful fabrics.

These headboards look like two giant cushions—and they are very comfortable.

A padded headboard in a very traditional shape.

A ruched, traditional-shaped headboard.

Wooden

Traditional carved bedframes come in a variety of styles.

Country-style wooden bedframes.

Contemporary

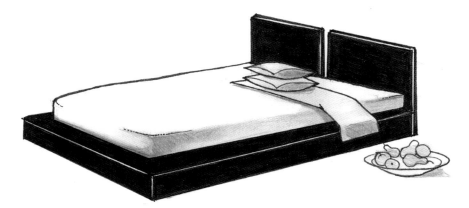

Modern wooden bedframe with two headboards.

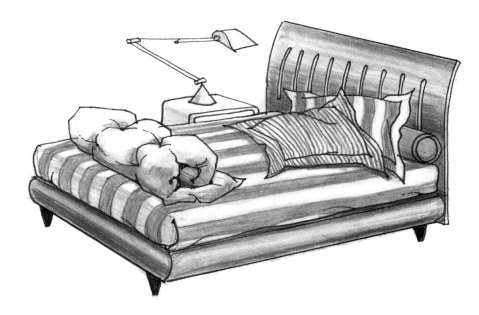

Slotted wooden headboard with a curved top.

Ebony bedframe with curved headboard and square
feet for an Oriental look.

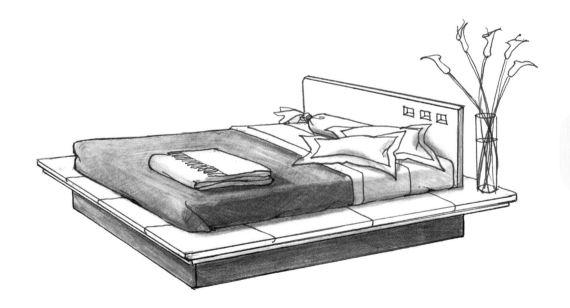

Contemporary bedframe with wooden surround.

Iron

Traditional iron bedstead with brass finials.

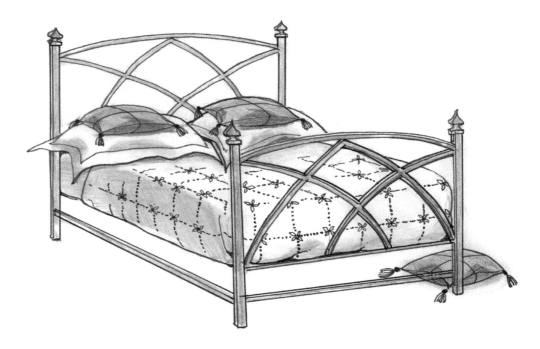

Modern version of the traditional metal bedstead.

Iron bedstead with brass detailing.

Wrought iron bedstead with pretty leaf details.

Iron

High posts at the bedhead to hold drapes.

Cast floral detailing in typical antique French style.

A modern four-poster looks just as good without any drapery.

Or you can add drapes for a softer look.

Coronas

The crystal fringe on the corona and bed drapery is repeated on the bed throw.

This corona has a triple pleat heading with square buttons and deep fringe.

The fabric used for this pinch-pleated corona is also used to line the bed drapery.

A light and pretty corona of wrought metal, with French-style voile curtains.

The classic corona looks best in a heritage property.

A formal daybed with heavily fringed corona and soft drapes.

Half testers

Bold floral drapes and ribbon borders give this half tester a more contemporary look.

The triangle point-edged pelmet with tassels evokes a medieval feel.

Traditional half tester with carved pelmet, heavy drapes and tasseled tie-backs.

A simplified traditional look, with drapes. The deep fringe on the valance is repeated on the bedcover.

Ostrich feathers and a heavily carved and tented pelmet give an opulent look to this half tester.

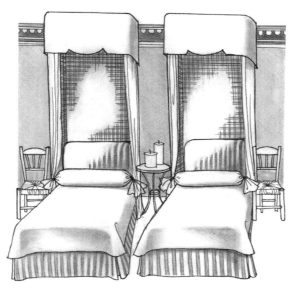

A pair of half tester beds in simple fabrics—a modern treatment that would not look out of place in a very traditional interior.

Traditional four-posters

Traditional four-posters are so over-the-top anyway that you can get away with using lots of wonderful trim.

Heavy crystal fringe accentuates the curving shape of the valance. The rope of the tie-backs is also used to trim the drapes, headboard, bolster and bedcover.

Four-poster with full drapes only at the bedhead for a less overpowering effect.

Some wooden four-posters have such beautifully turned pillars that it would be a crime to hide them with drapery.

The outline shape of the pelmet to this four-poster echoes the carving on the headboard.

Soft unstructured drapes and a tented ceiling contrast with the bold masculine posts of this ebony four-poster.

Pretty fabric twisted loosely around the posts and allowed to pool on the floor for a softer, more feminine look.

Modern four-posters

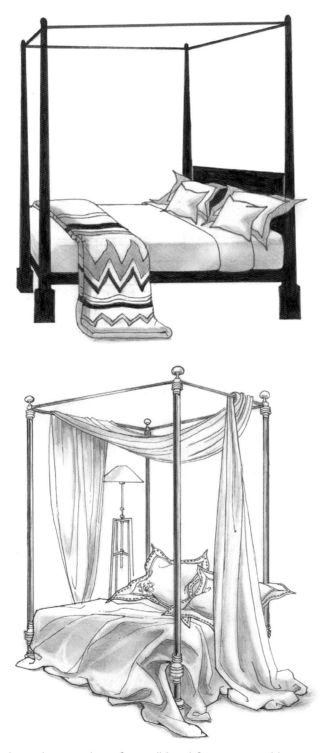

A simple ebony four-poster.

A metal frame creates a stunning look.

A modern version of a traditional four-poster, with muslin drapes.

This bamboo four-poster
echoes Far Eastern designs.

A Japanese-inspired metal frame.

Canopy

A draped canopy.

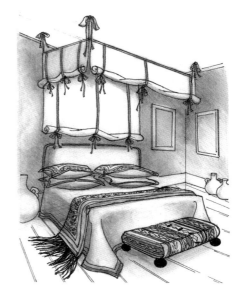

An imaginative way to use mosquito netting.

Traditional mosquito netting.

A double headboard with simple canopy.

The end of the canopy can be rolled down.

A really original canopy, made from chains and draped fabric.

Children's

A canopy over a child's cot creates a small, private world.

Wooden cots can be carved into all sorts of shapes—such as this teddy bear cot.

Ribbons, lace and a throw with a knotted fringe for this charming four-poster.

Boldly striped bedcover and football motifs make this the quintessential boy's room.

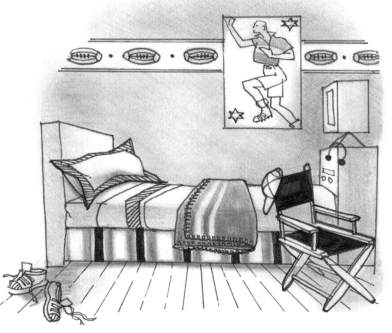

Children's

The shades create a great hideaway when down, but can be pulled up and out of the way. The bed itself contains plenty of storage for childhood treasures.

Child-size wooden four-poster.

An alcove bed is ideal for a child's room and can be dressed as a seating unit during the daytime.

A bunk bed over a study area is a compact and practical use of space.

Children's bedrooms

Three-tiered curtains using a different fabric for each tier.

A rod pocket heading with lace inserts.

A single panel with a band of wallpaper to match the motif on the wall.

A box-pleated heading with studs and checked lining to match the wallpaper.

Children's bedrooms

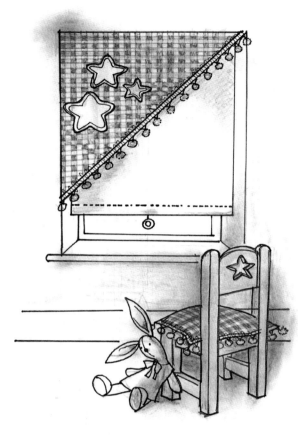

A pretty window treatment with a roller shade behind it.

This linen fold is placed over the recessed window.

An iron shepherd's pole with tiny pinch-pleated heading.

A casual heading on the drapes and a pointed soft pelmet decorated with bells.

Accessories

Introduction to accessories...

Accessorizing with style...
Sometimes it is the accessories that just make the scheme. If you have a fairly bland background palette, colorful accessories can make all the difference. And you can change them easily at little expense.

Table covers

These are easy to make and can be layered with several cloths or even just be a simple round piece of fabric perhaps with some kind of trim on the edge. They can be lined and even interlined to allow them to fall well—but this is for formal room settings, the trend now is for a more casual look. The following pages will give you some ideas.

Screens

Screens are very useful to divide a room, create a cozy corner, protect you from a draught or just to add a touch of extra decoration to a room. They are the latest accessory and are very handy in a whole host of situations. Hand painted or upholstered, in leather or in silk, there is no end to the combinations and their versatility.

Pillows

Pillows continue to be popular and you can never have too many of them. They do tend to be larger now and scatter pillows are a thing of the past.

I tend to try to find a theme for the pillows so that they tie in with the decor but don't look too contrived. For instance, if they are on a big settee with blankets thrown over them for a casual look I would have some knit ones and perhaps a couple of suede ones all in muted colors—I hate bright pillows!

Throws

Throws were originally meant to be rugs to throw over you if you were feeling a bit chilly, but now they are everywhere and come in all shapes and sizes. You can buy inexpensive ones, or those costing a fortune. I have a simple cashmere rug in London and a Welsh blanket in the country—nothing too pretentious for me!

Rugs

Rugs are my most favorite accessory. I prefer to have wide plank wooden floors everywhere in a flat or a house. In this way you can cover the floors with wonderful pure wool rugs and change the rugs every so often if you get bored with them.

Most stores have a huge supply of rugs from countries around the world—there is something to suit every taste. If you are working on a large project, such as a hotel, you can always have bespoke ones made—and there are companies who can make one-off designs for smaller projects, but at a price, of course.

Flowers

Flowers can change the feel of a room. They bring color into the room if that is what is needed or they can "pretty" a room up if that is what is missing.

Personally I do dislike silk flowers, but they are sometimes quite amazing. If they are used sparingly and mixed in with something natural—say autumn leaves, for instance—the effect does look very respectable.

Table covers

A collection of table covers, which can be made in mixed fabrics or perhaps in the same fabric as any drapes or pillows in the room.

Accessories

Mix prints and add beads to give some added interest—but remember that if you include any trims, the table covers must be dry cleaned.

Screens

Screens are useful for many reasons—I use them
sometimes instead of curtains, to keep out a draught or
to make a picture.

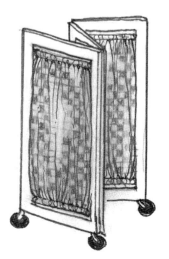

Accessories

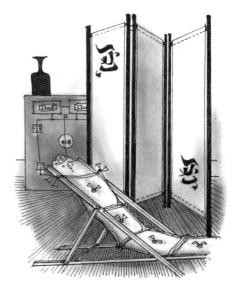

Pillows and throws

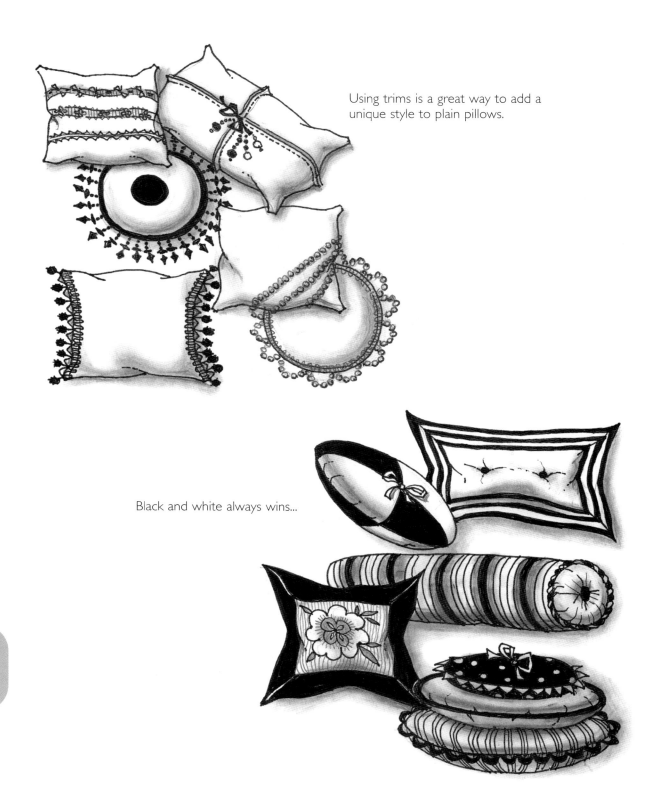

Using trims is a great way to add a unique style to plain pillows.

Black and white always wins...

254

Cotton checks, polka dots and floral prints are the essence of country style.

Throws and Welsh blankets are ideal to cover up boring fabrics and add instant chic.

Pillows

Black Russian braid is ideal to create your own designs. Experiment with frogging, lacing, appliqué and bows.

Animal prints add an exotic touch.

256

You can't really beat a classic Missoni print; it's a very distinguished style that will be a classic for many generations to come.

Rustic tweeds are ideal for the country house look, and combine well with bullion fringe, giant buttons and leather straps.

Flowers

Flowers add instant dressing to any scheme. Match the selection to the interior style—here bold flowers are teamed with a wide stripe wallpaper.

Create interest in a dull corner by adding delicate blossom in a glass vase.

Three small arrangements in a row can look better than one larger arrangement.

Rugs

A dramatic rug design like this looks best in a plain interior with no clutter to detract from its impact.

There is a wide range of styles available on the market—from simple stripes to traditional floral, and all combinations in between.

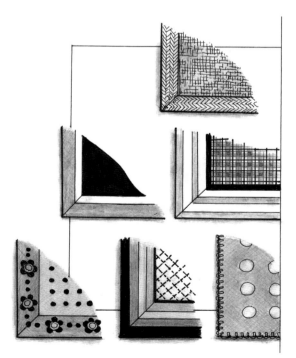

Borders add a finishing touch to a rug and can be plain or patterned.

Skills and Techniques

Measuring

Make sure you use a metal retractable measure to avoid making mistakes at this point when accurate measuring is vital. Decisions must be made before you measure, such as whether you will have a pole, tracking concealed by a covered lathe, a pelmet or a simple shade.

To measure accurately you should have the pole or whichever type of drapery tracking in position, in order to measure the drop (length) of the drape correctly. Generally these are fixed about 8 in (20 cm) above the architrave, but this does vary greatly depending on the position of the window to the ceiling. Wooden poles should be 2½ in (6.3 cm) in diameter if the drapes are long and can be as thin as 1 in (2.5 cm) for voile drapes (sheers) or short ones.

Be sure to check the following...

- ▶ You have sketched a flat drawing of your window so that you can put the measurements on the outline for accuracy.
- ▶ Make sure you have chosen the right design for the window.
- ▶ Choose a suitable pole or tracking.
- ▶ Are you having a pelmet or valance? Check this is right for the window—will you block out too much light?
- ▶ Decide on the type of heading for your drapes.
- ▶ Check which way your windows open—if they open into the room be sure your chosen window coverings will clear the window when it is open.
- ▶ It is best to have a place to stack the drapes on either side of the window when the drapes are open, so you do not lose too much light during the day. Your pole should be fixed the whole width including the "stack backs".

- ▶ If you have to hang the drapes from the ceiling, be sure to find a fixing in a beam that will be strong enough to take the weight.
- ▶ Start to measure up, using a retractable metal measure.
- ▶ The drapery pole, tracking or pelmet board should be in place before you take any measurements.
- ▶ As a general rule tracks or poles should be fixed about 8 in (20 cm) above the architrave, but this does vary greatly depending on the relationship of the window to the ceiling—this is where common sense comes into it!
- ▶ If you are using a pole for your drapes be sure to use the right thickness. If the drapes are long the pole should be at least 2½ in (6.3 cm) in diameter. For voiles or short drapes the pole can be thinner—maybe 1 in (2.5 cm)—but I would rather have the pole a bit too thick than too mean looking.

Sewing tools

To achieve good results in your drapery-making projects you will need a few pieces of equipment, but most of the items are not expensive and you probably already have most of them in your sewing kit. Start by purchasing the essentials: needles, pins, tape measure, your choice of marking tools, dressmaker's shears, seam ripper. Buy the best you can afford and add other items as you need them.

You will need a sewing machine—although it is feasible to hand-sew drapes, it is very hard work and will take a really long time, so why bother? If you don't have a sewing machine, try to borrow one. You only need a basic model—computerized functions and embroidery stitches are not necessary.

Essential equipment

Sewing machine – the most expensive piece of sewing equipment you will need to purchase is a sewing machine, so if you plan to buy one it is worth taking time to be sure you end up with one you like to use. If you don't have one already try to borrow one to make your first drapes—this will give you some idea of which functions you will actually need and which ones you will not. There is no point in paying for complex features that you may not understand and will probably never use. Try out different machines in the showroom and take full advantage of any professional instruction that may be offered. The instruction book will explain your specific machine, but most have some common features.

Dressmaker's scissors – these have blades at an angle to the handles, so the blade can slide along the worksurface when cutting and not lift the fabric much, which allows for more accurate cutting.

Pinking shears – these shears have notched blades so they cut a zigzag line, which is useful to trim raw seam edges to prevent fraying.

Embroidery scissors – the short, sharp blades of embroidery scissors are designed to trim threads. Do not use your fabric shears for this, as it will eventually blunt the blade.

Tape measure (flexible and metal retractable) – a flexible tape measure is useful to take measurements of fabric. Use a plastic or fiberglass one—the cloth ones are prone to stretch over time. The metal retractable tape is the ideal tool to take measurements of windows, as you can extend the measure way above your head.

Tailor's chalk – solid chalk for marking fabric often comes in a triangular shape for ease of use and can be used to make a range of line thicknesses.

Pins with colored heads – the large colored heads of these pins make them easy to spot when you need to remove them. Buy those with glass heads rather than plastic, which may melt if caught with an iron.

Sewing needles (all sizes) – ordinary sewing needles are commonly called sharps. Keep a selection in a range of sizes. Change your sewing machine needle regularly—a blunt needle will cause stitching problems.

Thimble – many people do not like to use a thimble, but if you do a lot of sewing you will soon get used to using it and it will save your fingers from damage.

Seam ripper – this special tool is invaluable—it has a sharp prong to push into stitches and a short curved blade to cut through them.

Thread – thread comes in a range of fibers, both natural and synthetic, and in many colors. It also comes in different thicknesses—the thicker threads are normally used for things like topstitching, where the stitches are designed to be seen as a feature.

Hem weights – these cone-like weights are sometimes known as penny or hem weights. They are used at the bottom corners and at the bottom of each joined seam. A small size is suitable for lightweight drapes, the larger heavier size is better for heavy fabric and full length drapes.

Touch and close tape (Velcro®) – this consists of two layers: a "hook" side, which is a piece of fabric covered with tiny hooks, and a "loop" side, which is covered with even smaller loops. When the two sides are pressed together, the hooks catch in the loops and hold the pieces together.

Eyelet hole kit – this consists of a punch to make the hole, and a setting tool to place and lock the two halves of the eyelet rings to seal the edges of the hole.

Tracing paper (I use parchment cooking paper) – useful to trace designs or transfer markings.

Steam iron – you will need to press seams open during the making process, and press hems. You can use your regular ironing surface and steam iron for this.

Weights – These are used to hold down lightweight fabrics while you cut them out.

Measuring for drapes/curtains

Measuring cut length drapes

For short drapes, measure from the ring on pole or track to 5 in (13 cm) below the sill ①. For long drapes, measure from the ring on pole or track to the floor ②, but add extra if you want the drapes to break on the floor.

Pelmets or valances—fix the pelmet board at the same height as you would a pole. The depth of the pelmet or valance should, as a rough guide, be one-sixth of the total height of the drapes, so divide the drapery height by six to find the correct depth ③. Add 5 in (13 cm) to allow for your heading and hem.

Measuring drape width

Measure between the architraves ④ and add on an extra 12 in (30 cm) on each side to allow for stack-backs ⑤. Remember to add seam allowances.

Measuring up for shades

Fix shades approximately 8 in (20 cm) above the architrave to allow as much light as possible into the room. Measure the width between the architraves and add 2 in (5 cm) each side ⑥. To work out the length, measure the length of the window and add 8 in (20 cm) above the architrave plus 1 in (2.5 cm) below the sill ⑦.

Measuring up for drapes and shades in recess

Measure the length from the top to the bottom of the recess. Measure the width of the recess. If you choose shades, always remember to check the measurements at the top, middle and bottom as windows can be irregular. If the window is very small, it is preferable to hang drapes outside the recess to avoid losing too much light, or use a swing arm to hang the drapes.

Measuring up for swags and tails

For the swag length, measure the width of the pelmet board that is going to carry your tracking and add approximately 16 in (40 cm). To calculate the swag depth, multiply the required length by two. The inner edge of the tail should be the same length as the swag. The outer edge should be about three-quarters of the total drapery length.

Calculating fabric requirements

Divide the drapery width by the width of your fabric to find the number of fabric drops (lengths) required. Decide on the fullness you require. Traditional drapes should have 2–3 widths of fabric, unless the fabric is very thick, and the more contemporary styles are generally about two widths of fullness—see the section on fabric quantities on pages 266–8. Obviously panels have no fullness at all. Multiply the number of drops by the cut length measurement to find the required amount of fabric (see table on page 266). If your fabric has a pattern, allow one EXTRA pattern repeat for each drop.

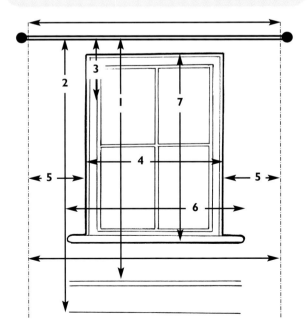

Measuring for shades

Face fix

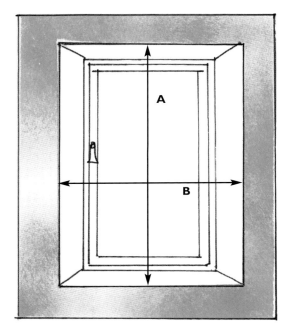

Recessed window

A The drop (length) from the top of the architrave to the sill.

B The drop (length) from 8 in (20 cm) above the architrave to just below the sill.

C The width if the shade is to be fixed on the architrave.

D The width if the shade is to overlap on either side.

E The top point is where a pole, pelmet or valance should be fixed—approx. 8 in (20 cm). The bottom point is the drop of the pelmet or valance.

A The drop (length).

B The width—take the measurement at the top, middle and near the bottom as windows can vary in a recess.

Skills and
Techniques

Fabric quantities for drapes/curtains

2½ x heading fullness
12 in (30 cm) heading and hem allowance, 2 x 2¾ in (7 cm) overlaps and 2 x 3¼ in (8 cm)
returns (sides), includes seam allowances

Measurements in imperial

Length of track or pole up to

48 in fabric	22 in	3 ft 4 in	5 ft	6 ft 8 in	8 ft 2 in	9 ft 6 in	11 ft	12 ft 7 in	14 ft
54 in fabric	28 in	4 ft	5 ft 10 in	7 ft 7 in	9 ft 4 in	11 ft	12 ft 9 in	14 ft 7 in	16 ft 5 in
60 in fabric	32 in	4 ft 8 in	6 ft 7 in	8 ft 6 in	10 ft 4 in	12 ft 4 in	14 ft 3 in	16 ft	5.50

No. of widths	2	3	4	5	6	7	8	9	10
Finished Length									
71 in	4 5/8 yd	7 yd	9 1/4 yd	11 1/2 yd	13 7/8 yd	16 1/8 yd	18 3/8 yd	20 3/4 yd	23 yd
75 in	4 7/8 yd	7 1/4 yd	9 5/8 yd	12 1/8 yd	14 1/8 yd	16 7/8 yd	19 1/4 yd	21 3/4 yd	24 1/8 yd
79 in	5 1/8 yd	7 5/8 yd	10 1/8 yd	12 5/8 yd	15 1/8 yd	17 5/8 yd	20 1/8 yd	22 5/8 yd	25 1/4 yd
83 in	5 1/4 yd	7 7/8 yd	10 1/2 yd	13 1/8 yd	15 3/4 yd	18 3/8 yd	21 yd	23 5/8 yd	26 1/4 yd
87 in	5 1/2 yd	8 1/4 yd	11 yd	13 3/4 yd	16 1/2 yd	19 1/4 yd	21 7/8 yd	24 5/8 yd	27 3/8 yd
91 in	5 3/4 yd	8 5/8 yd	11 3/8 yd	14 1/4 yd	17 1/8 yd	20 yd	22 3/4 yd	25 5/8 yd	28 1/2 yd
94 in	6 yd	8 7/8 yd	11 7/8 yd	14 7/8 yd	17 3/4 yd	20 3/4 yd	23 5/8 yd	26 5/8 yd	29 5/8 yd
98 in	6 1/8 yd	9 1/4 yd	12 1/4 yd	15 3/8 yd	18 3/8 yd	21 3/4 yd	24 1/2 yd	27 5/8 yd	30 5/8 yd
102 in	6 3/8 yd	9 5/8 yd	12 3/4 yd	15 7/8 yd	19 1/8 yd	22 1/4 yd	25 3/8 yd	28 5/8 yd	31 3/4 yd
106 in	6 5/8 yd	9 7/8 yd	13 1/8 yd	16 1/2 yd	19 3/4 yd	23 yd	26 1/4 yd	29 5/8 yd	32 7/8 yd
110 in	6 7/8 yd	10 1/4 yd	13 5/8 yd	17 yd	20 3/8 yd	23 3/4 yd	27 1/8 yd	30 1/2 yd	34 1/8 yd
114 in	7 yd	10 1/2 yd	14 yd	17 1/2 yd	21 yd	24 1/2 yd	28 yd	31 1/2 yd	35 yd
118 in	7 1/4 yd	10 7/8 yd	14 1/8 yd	18 1/8 yd	21 3/4 yd	25 1/4 yd	28 7/8 yd	32 1/2 yd	36 1/8 yd
122 in	7 1/2 yd	11 1/4 yd	14 7/8 yd	18 1/2 yd	22 3/8 yd	25 5/8 yd	29 3/4 yd	33 1/2 yd	37 1/4 yd
126 in	7 3/4 yd	11 1/2 yd	15 3/8 yd	19 1/4 yd	23 yd	26 7/8 yd	30 5/8 yd	34 1/2 yd	38 3/8 yd
130 in	7 7/8 yd	11 7/8 yd	15 3/4 yd	19 3/4 yd	23 5/8 yd	27 5/8 yd	31 1/2 yd	35 1/2 yd	39 3/8 yd
134 in	8 1/8 yd	12 1/4 yd	16 1/4 yd	20 1/4 yd	24 3/8 yd	28 3/8 yd	32 3/8 yd	36 1/2 yd	40 1/2 yd
136 in	8 3/8 yd	12 1/2 yd	16 5/8 yd	20 7/8 yd	25 yd	29 1/8 yd	33 1/4 yd	37 1/2 yd	41 5/8 yd

To use this chart:

1 Find your fabric width at top right in the first column. Go along the line to the right of the fabric width to find the nearest measurement to the width of your track or pole—if this falls between two measurements, use the larger one.

2 Find the number of fabric widths you need by looking directly below your track or pole measurement in the No. of widths line.

3 The column below the number of widths shows the amount of fabric required to achieve a finished length of drapes as shown in the column on the far left.

Fabric quantities for valances

2½ x heading fullness
Valances can have more fullness in them than the accompanying drapes.
This fullness is suitable for most decorative headings, especially hand
box-pleated valances (although some machine tapes require 3 x fullness)
and smocked-headed valances.

6 in (15 cm) for heading and hem allowance, includes seam allowances
2 x 6 in (15 cm) returns for either pelmet board or valance rail

Measurements in imperial

Length of pelmet board or valance rail up to

48 in fabric	24 in	3 ft 5 in	5 ft	6 ft 7 in	8 ft 2 in	9 ft 8 in	11 ft 2 in	12 ft 9 in	14 ft 3 in
54 in fabric	28 in	4 ft 1 in	5 ft 11 in	7 ft 8 in	9 ft 4 in	11 ft 2 in	12 ft 11 in	14 ft 9 in	16 ft 5 in
60 in fabric	33 in	4 ft 9 in	6 ft 7 in	8 ft 6 in	10 ft 6 in	12 ft 6 in	14 ft 3 in	16 ft 3 in	18 ft 2 in

No. of widths	2	3	4	5	6	7	8	9	10
Finished Length									
12 in	1 yd	1½ yd	2 yd	2½ yd	3 yd	3½ yd	4 yd	4½ yd	5 yd
14 in	1⅛ yd	1¾ yd	2¼ yd	2¾ yd	3⅜ yd	4 yd	4⅜ yd	5 yd	5½ yd
16 in	1¼ yd	1⅞ yd	2½ yd	3 yd	3¾ yd	4¼ yd	4⅞ yd	5½ yd	6⅛ yd
18 in	1⅜ yd	2 yd	2¾ yd	3⅜ yd	4 yd	4⅝ yd	5¼ yd	6 yd	6⅝ yd
20 in	1½ yd	2¼ yd	2⅞ yd	3⅝ yd	4½ yd	5 yd	5¾ yd	6½ yd	6.50
22 in	1⅝ yd	2⅜ yd	3⅛ yd	4 yd	4⅝ yd	5⅜ yd	6⅛ yd	7 yd	7⅛ yd
24 in	1¾ yd	2½ yd	3⅜ yd	4⅛ yd	5 yd	5¾ yd	6⅝ yd	7½ yd	7¾ yd
26 in	1¾ yd	2¾ yd	3½ yd	4⅜ yd	5¼ yd	6⅛ yd	7 yd	7⅞ yd	8¼ yd
28 in	1⅞ yd	2⅞ yd	3¾ yd	4¾ yd	5⅝ yd	6½ yd	7½ yd	8⅜ yd	8¾ yd
30 in	2 yd	3 yd	4 yd	5 yd	6 yd	7 yd	7⅞ yd	8⅞ yd	9⅜ yd
32 in	2⅛ yd	3⅛ yd	4¼ yd	5¼ yd	6¼ yd	7⅜ yd	8⅜ yd	9⅜ yd	9⅞ yd
33 in	2¼ yd	3⅜ yd	4⅜ yd	5½ yd	6⅝ yd	7¾ yd	8¾ yd	9⅞ yd	10½ yd
35 in	2⅜ yd	3½ yd	4⅝ yd	5¾ yd	7 yd	8⅛ yd	9¼ yd	10⅜ yd	11½ yd
37 in	2½ yd	3⅝ yd	4⅞ yd	6⅛ yd	7¼ yd	8½ yd	9⅝ yd	10⅞ yd	12⅛ yd
40 in	2⅝ yd	3⅞ yd	5⅛ yd	6⅜ yd	7⅝ yd	8⅞ yd	10⅛ yd	11⅜ yd	12⅝ yd

To use this chart:

1. Find your fabric width at top right in the first column. Go along the line to the right of the fabric width to find the nearest measurement to the width of your track or pole—if this falls between two measurements, use the larger one.
2. Find the number of fabric widths you need by looking directly below your track or pole measurement in the No. of widths line.
3. The column below the number of widths shows the amount of fabric required to achieve a finished length of valances as shown in the column on the far left.

Fabric quantities for swags and tails

Swags

Swags can be butted together or overlapped. A small overlap creates a pronounced scallop-shaped hemline. When swags are overlapped center to center, the hemline forms a shallow wavy shape.

Quantities given per swag, finished depth either 17¾ in (45 cm) or 21¾ in (55cm)
Assumes 54 in (137cm)-wide fabric, includes seam allowances

Measurements in inches and yards

Swag width	Fabric quantity (No. of widths x cut drop)	Hem measurement for fringe quantities
24 in	1¼ yd (1 x 1¼ yd)	1¾ yd
28 in	1¼ yd (1 x 1¼ yd)	1⅞ yd
32 in	1¼ yd (1 x 1¼ yd)	1⅞ yd
35 in	1¼ yd (1 x 1¼ yd)	1⅞ yd
40 in	1¼ yd (1 x 1¼ yd)	2 yd
43 in	1¼ yd (1 x 1¼ yd)	2 yd
47 in	1¼ yd (1 x 1¼ yd)	2⅛ yd
51 in	2½ yd (2 x 1¼ yd)	2¼ yd
55 in	2¾ yd (2 x 1⅜ yd)	2¼ yd
59 in	2¾ yd (2 x 1⅜ yd)	2⅜ yd
63 in	2¾ yd (2 x 1⅜ yd)	2½ yd
67 in	2¾ yd (2 x 1⅜ yd)	2⅝ yd

Tails

Quantities given per pair, 6 in (15 cm) pelmet board return
Assumes 54 in (137 cm)-wide fabric, includes seam allowances

Measurements in inches and yards

Length of tail up to	Fabric	Contrast lining	Hem measurement for fringe quantities
35 in – straight tail	2¼ yd (2 x 1⅛ yd)	2¼ yd	2⅝ yd
43 in – straight tail	2¾ yd (2 x 1⅜ yd)	2¾ yd	2¾ yd
53 in – straight tail	3¼ yd (2 x 1⅝ yd)	3¼ yd	3⅝ yd
53 in – cone shape	3¼ yd (2 x 1⅞ yd)	3¾ yd	4⅛ yd
65 in – straight tail	4 yd (2 x 2 yd)	4 yd	4 yd
65 in – cone shape	4½ yd (2 x 2¼ yd)	4½ yd	4⅜ yd

Fabric quantities for Roman shades

Roman shades can be fitted inside or outside the window reveal and are a smart form of window dressing where wall space around the window is restricted.

6 in (15 cm) for heading and hem allowance, includes seam allowances
12 in (30 cm) fabric to cover batten

Measurements in feet and inches

	Finished width of shade up to	Finished width of shade up to
48 in fabric	43 in	7 ft 3 in
54 in fabric	49 in	8 ft 6 in
60 in fabric	53 in	9 ft 2 in
	Finished length	**Finished length**
	+ 18 in	+ 18 in x 2 widths

To use this chart:

1 Find your fabric width at top right in the first column. The first column to the right of the fabric width shows the maximum finished width shade you can make with one width of fabric, the second column shows the maxiumn finished width shade you can make with two widths.

2 To find the length of fabric required take the finished length of the shade, multiply by the number of widths of fabric required and add 18 in for heading, hem and to cover the batten.

Sewing skills

Preparing to cut and pattern match

Take time to check you have everything you need before making a start. Double-check that you remembered to allow enough fabric for pattern repeats before cutting—see measuring section.

1 Cutting out—cut fabric on long clean surface. Check all lengths of fabric are running the same way. Use a set square and metal ruler to mark a straight line across the fabric. Measure the first drop down the selvage line and mark your top and bottom with pins, making sure your next drop matches at repeats. Continue this way for rest of widths—part widths go on the outer edges.

2 Pattern match—put the two selvages together and line up print facing you on both sides as in the diagram—pop a pin in at the top and bottom to hold in place as a marker.

Tips

Use a large stitch when sewing seams as a small tight seam causes pulling and puckering and doesn't always press out.

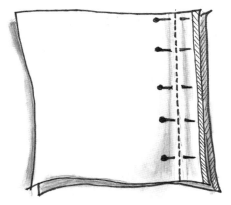

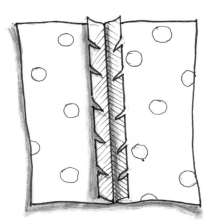

3 Pin and sew—lay your two fabric lengths down on your sewing table face to face—selvage to selvage. Place the pins horizontally as in the diagram. Allow 1in (2.5 cm) from selvage for sewing line for a plain fabric. If it is a print then the sewing line depends on the pattern match. Machine straight over your pins—don't worry, they won't break nor will your machine needle! If you don't believe it you can use a running stitch instead.

4 Snip seams—go quite close to machine line but not through it. Snipping stops any puckering or gathering on seams—essential when machining shaped parts of a drape. Press seam open with a fairly hot iron.

Skills and Techniques

Stitches

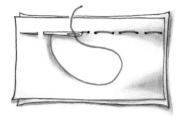

Running, gathering and basting stitch
Stitch used for basting or gathering.

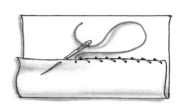

Hemming stitch
Used to hem and to stop fraying.

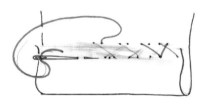

Herringbone stitch
Used for hems or to neaten seams.

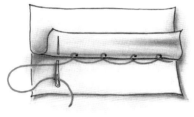

Loose stitch
Sometimes used to loosely attach lining to fabric.

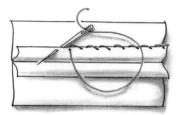

Overlocking stitch
Used to stop fabric fraying on hand-sewn drapes.

Blanket stitch
Use thick wool or thread for this.

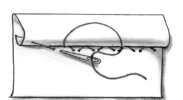

Blind stitching
For sewing on ribbons and braids by hand.

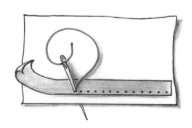

Locking stitch
Used for joining interlining to the main fabric.

Unlined drapes with mitering

1 Measure the window as shown on page 264 and cut your fabric accordingly, remembering to add seam allowances for hem, headings and side seams.

2 If you are using more than one width of fabric for each drape, pin, baste and machine stitch the widths together.

3 Overlock the edges of all seams to stop the fabric fraying—press the seams open.

4 On both sides of one drape make a double hem by turning the edges in TWICE by 1¼ in (3 cm) each time. Pin and baste these edges to within 2¾ in (7 cm) from the top of the drape and 6 in (15 cm) from the bottom.

5 Turn up the hem allowance by 6 in (15 cm) TWICE and press flat. Open out the folds and then fold the bottom corners across diagonally to meet the seam line to make a miter.

6 Cut away the excess fabric across the miter around ¼ in (5 mm) from the diagonal fold.

7 Fold the double hem back into place, then slip stitch the hem.

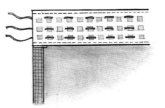

8 Turn over the top to the wrong side by enough to make the drape the finished length required. Stitch your chosen heading tape in place across the top.

9 Knot the loose cords at one end of the heading tape and pull on the cords at the other end to gather the fabric into even pleats across the width of the curtain. Knot the cords, wind the excess around your fingers and tuck behind the heading tape. Slot the hooks onto the tape—there is usually a choice of levels, depending on whether you are hanging the drape from a pole or a track. Repeat steps 4 to 9 for the other drape.

Locked-in Lining

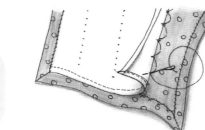

1 Make up the drape as described above.

2 Lock-stitch is used on hand-made drapes to attach a separate lining loosely to the main fabric. The lining is laid on the drapes with wrong sides together (both already hemmed). The leading edge is hemmed, then, at 18 in (45 cm) intervals across the width, the lining is folded back. From the top almost to the bottom of the lining, a long, loose stitch is made catching the drape and then the lining. This is followed by a small back-stitch on lining.

Lined drapes

1 Measure, cut and make up your main drapery fabric as in steps 1–3 on page 272.

2 Cut the lining the same size as your finished drapes will be (in other words DO NOT ADD ANY SEAM ALLOWANCES AT THE SIDES, OR ALLOWANCES FOR HEADING OR HEM!).

3 If you are using more than one width of fabric for each drape lining, pin, baste and machine stitch all of the widths together.

4 Make a double hem on the lining, turning the hem up by 1¼ in (3 cm) each time, then machine the hem and press. Press under the raw edges by 1 in (2.5 cm) on the sides and top of the lining only.

5 Place the lining centrally onto the drape with right sides together. Pin into position and then stitch the seams on each side only.

6 Turn the drape right side out and press down the side seams.

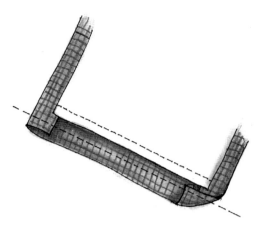

7 Turn up the hem allowance twice on the main drape fabric by 6 in (15 cm) each time and press flat. Open out and then press the two corners to the seam line to make a miter.

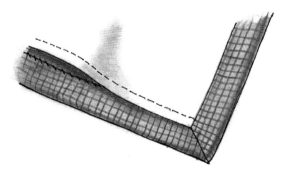

8 Slip stitch the hem. Add your chosen heading tape as in steps 8 and 9 on page 272. Repeat steps 4 to 8 to line the other drape.

Tips

To stop the lining flapping around behind the drapes, you can always put a loose chain stitch here and there.

Tie heading

1 Cut out the fabric for the drapes and for the ties—which should each be about 1 in (2.5 cm) wide and 8 in (20 cm) long.

2 Make the drapes as for unlined drapes, steps 1 to 8 (see page 272), but do not add heading tape.

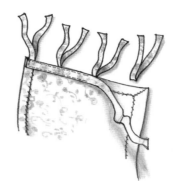

3 Make the ties by pressing the fabric in half and then in quarters. Press in the short ends and machine-stitch all around the ties. Fold each tie in half.

4 Lay the drape down with the right sides facing upward and lay the folded ties equally spaced apart across the top. Pin the ties in place.

5 Cut a strip of fabric the width of one drape and about 4 in (10 cm) deep as a facing and turn under all edges. Place the facing along the top edge of the drape covering the base of the ties and stitch all around to hold the ties in place. Repeat steps 4 and 5 on the other drape.

Tab heading

1 Cut out the main fabric for the drapes and the tabs.

2 Cut the facing for both drapes—a strip of fabric the width of one drape and about 4 in (10 cm) deep for each.

3 Make the drapes as for unlined drapes, steps 1 to 8 (see page 272), but do not add heading tape.

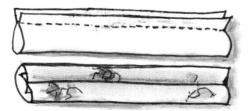

4 Make the tabs by cutting a length of fabric about 8 in (20 cm) long for each. Fold in half lengthways, right sides together, and stitch. Turn the tube right side out.

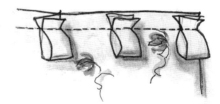

5 Fold each tab in half and lay at equal intervals along the top edge of the drape, with folds pointing down. Baste the tabs in place.

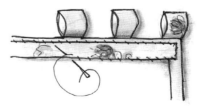

6 Fold the tabs so they are pointing upwards and press in place. Turn under all the edges of the facing and lay it along the top of the drape, wrong sides together, and covering the attached ends of the tabs. Slip stitch the facing all around to neaten.

Skills and Techniques

Italian stringing

1 Put up your pole and fix the cleat about one-third of the way up from the floor.

2 Cut the top and contrast fabrics for the drape to the same size with usual top, hem and side seam allowances.

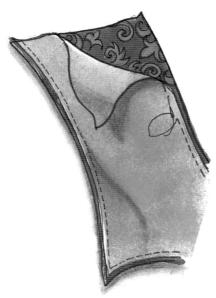

3 Lay the top and the contrast right sides together. Pin, baste and then machine stitch together leaving just the top open to form a "bag". Turn the drape right side out through the top and press the seams.

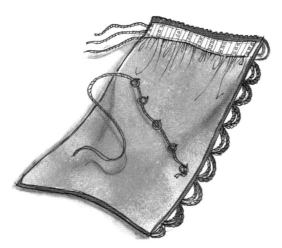

4 To apply the heading tape, fold down the top of the drape by about 1¼ in (3 cm). Check your required length and if the drape is too long or short, adjust the fold here to achieve the correct length. Pin the chosen heading tape

½ in (1 cm) from the top. Baste and then machine stitch in place. Tie a knot in the cords of the tape and gather the drape to the required width, and then tie a bow in the loose cords. Make sure the pleats are even across the top.

5 Sew braid onto the leading edge of the drape.

6 Place the drape right side down and sew a cording ring on the contrast fabric at the leading edge, about one-third of the way down the drape. Sew another four or five rings to the contrast fabric running at a 45° angle towards the other edge of the drape, and about 20cm (8in) apart. Knot the cord onto the first ring and thread through the other rings—leave plenty of cord at the end to secure into a cleat on the wall.

7 Wind the excess cords from the heading tape around your fingers and tuck behind the end of the tape. Hang the drape in place, then pull up the stringing cord to pull the drape into an attractive curving shape. Secure the loose cord to the cleat in the wall.

Tips

Don't use a very heavy fabric for the drapes as the stringing is not that strong.

Skills and Techniques

Valance on a pelmet board

1 Cover the pelmet board—put into place together with the drapery track.

2 Staple the first side of the touch and close tape to the front of the pelmet board.

3 Cut the main drapery fabric to your measurements and make up as on page 273 (lined drapes). Put on heading tape as in steps 8 and 9 on page 272. Press, then put on your drapery hooks and hang the drapes.

4 Measure the actual width of the pelmet board plus the returns (sides) and cut a template in paper to this width. As a guide for the depth of your valance, cut the deepest section to about half the length of your main drapes. Fold the paper template in half to find the center line and then shape the bottom edge with a dotted line. Baste your template to the pelmet and check the proportions—adjust accordingly.

5 To make an elongated template for the fabric, simply multiply the actual width of the pelmet by 2.5 and add on the returns. Now take the center measurement off the original template and transfer this to the center of the elongated one; do the same at both ends and continue to take measurements at regular intervals, say every 4 in (10 cm). Then all you need to do is join up the dots and you have a shaped valance template (see diagrams on page 277 for examples).

Tips

Before you continue, look at the page opposite, where you will find some valance templates. When you have studied these and made your choice—proceed!

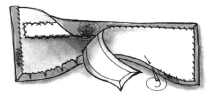

6 Pin your finished template on to your fabric and, remembering to add your seam allowances top and bottom, make a dotted line around the shape. Cut out—then repeat for lining. Press the seam allowances to the wrong side along all edges of the main fabric, clipping any curves and mitering the corners. Open out the top hem and stitch a strip of buckram underneath, then fold back. Pin and slip stitch the hems in place. Turn under the seam allowances around all edges of the lining, center it over the valance, wrong sides together, and slip stitch in place along all edges.

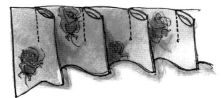

7 Work out how many goblets you will need for your valance width—as a guide I allow about 6 in (15 cm) for each goblet and the same for each gap between them. With the right side of the fabric facing you, fold over your 6 in (15 cm) pleat, baste and machine to just below the bottom edge of the buckram. Then secure the base of each goblet with a few stitches. Open up each goblet to make a "cup" and stuff with batting.

8 Sew on the fan edge trim. Knot and loop the rope at the base of the goblets. Stitch the other side of the touch and close tape to the back of the fabric about 1 in (2.5 cm) from the top and press the valance into place.

Valance templates

REMEMBER if the valances are gathered you must elongate the shapes to allow for the fabric fullness, so you will need to cut a second template to the finished size of the actual valance before gathering. Then you need to take the measurements indicated and transfer to the main diagram in order to arrive at the correct shape.

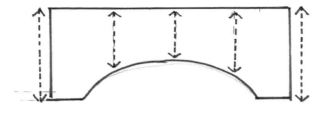

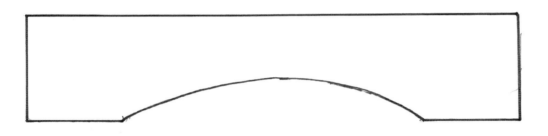

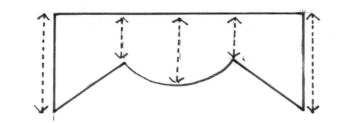

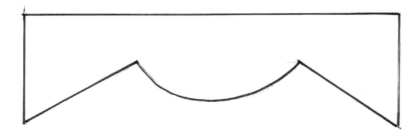

Roman shades

1 Cut your fabric to the exact size of the shade plus seam allowances—and the same for the lining.

2 Cover the pelmet board with matching fabric.

3 Staple a length of one half of the touch and close tape to the front edge of the pelmet board (see step 2 page 276).

4 Put the pelmet board in its place with the correct brackets.

5 Work on your main fabric first—press the sides and the bottom turnings under once, then put the main fabric to one side.

6 Press in the side turnings on the lining so it is about 2 in (5 cm) narrower than the main fabric.

7 Mark your lining with tailor's chalk exactly where you need the pockets for the dowel rods. As a rough guide, measure 4 in (10 cm) up from the bottom and that is where the first pocket should be—then one every 10–12 in (25 –30 cm). Make sure they are evenly distributed. Make your pockets by folding strips of fabric the width of the shade in half and then into quarters.

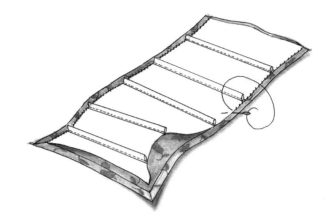

8 Machine each of the dowel rod pockets onto the lining in turn. Slide rounded wooden dowels into each pocket. To make up the shade, carefully slip stitch the lining to the main fabric along the sides and bottom.

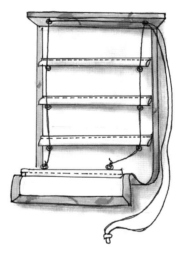

9 Add small brass rings to the edge of each pocket, in a line near each side of the shade. Screw two eyelet screws onto the underside of the pelmet board in line with the brass rings on the shade. Turn over the raw edge at the top of the shade and slip stitch a length of the second half of the touch and close tape to hide the raw edge. Press the tape to the length on the pelmet board to hang the shade.

10 Lastly, thread the cord through the rings as in the diagram—the diagram is from the window looking into the room, so is for a left hand pull shade—and thread the cord end onto the cord, before wrapping the cord around a cleat on the wall to secure.

Oriental shades

1 Cut the fabric the length of your window plus 10 in (25 cm) for the hems and 2 in (5 cm) for the sides.

2 Lay the fabric wrong side up and make a double hem down the sides by pressing under ¼ in (0.5 cm) and then another 1¼ in (3 cm).

3 Make a double hem at the top of the shade, turning under by 4 in (10 cm) and then another 4 in (10 cm). Press, baste and machine.

4 Mark your two sets of eyelet holes—place the outer set 2 in (5 cm) down from the top and 6 in (15 cm) from one side. The inner hole should be 4 in (10 cm) in from this one. Repeat on the other side.

5 Punch the four holes with a fairly large size eyelet hole.

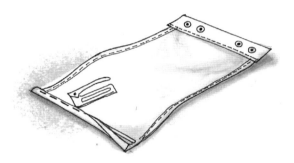

6 Place the dowel rod along the bottom, turn the raw edge of the shade under then fold it over the dowel and staple in place.

7 Slip stitch a length of the looped half of the touch and close tape to the reverse side of the top of the shade. Cover the batten with fabric, then attach the batten to its correct position over the window with long screws. Staple the other half of the touch and close tape to the batten.

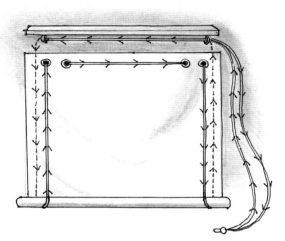

8 Screw the two eyelet screws onto the underside of the batten in line with the two outer eyelet holes on the shade. Attach the shade with the two sides of the touch and close tape. Now thread your cord starting from the cleat—just follow the arrows above.

Patterns for basic table covers

Plain

1 Measure your table from the center to the floor—double the measurement and add seam allowances. Lay your fabric on a flat surface—your fabric may be wide enough to cut the full circle, but if not then follow the diagram below.

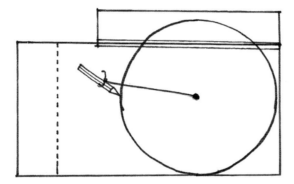

2 Once you have drawn your circle, cut the extra fabric and seam onto the edge of the main fabric as shown.

3 Press a double hem all the way around and, finally, machine the edge carefully.

Top and undercover

1 Make the undercover as for a plain table cover.

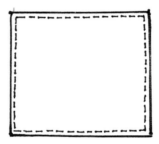

2 For the top cover, cut the fabric into a square. Press a double hem all around.

3 Miter the corners as on page 272 and baste. Lastly, machine all around the square and press.

Square

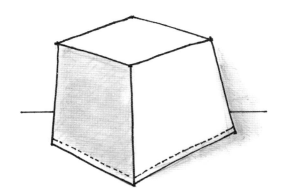

1 Take the measurements of the pieces shown in the diagrams below and draw the pieces on a piece of graph paper—allow a seam allowance on every edge.

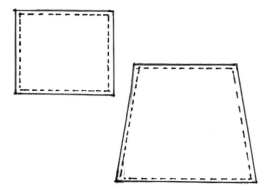

2 Pin, baste and sew together and cut away any excess fabric in the corners.

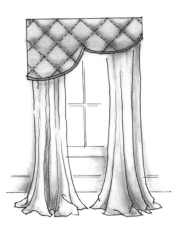

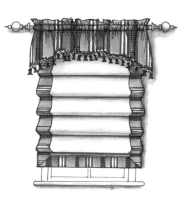
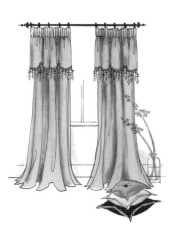
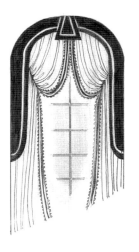

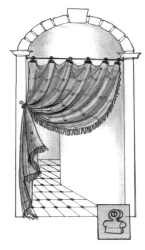

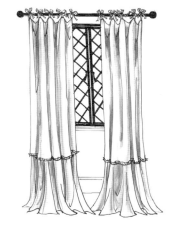

Glossary

abutted seam – a seam used to join non-woven interfacing, in which the two edges are butted together over a narrow band of lightweight fabric underlay and a line of wide zigzag machine stitching down the join holds the two pieces together.

anchor – to fix the end of a piece of yarn or thread, or attach a piece of fabric at one point, so it will not pull away from the main piece. Some stitchers begin sewing with a few small running stitches to anchor the thread, others prefer to knot the end so that it will not pull through the fabric.

architrave – a molded frame around the sides and top of a window or door.

basting – a technique used to temporarily hold layers of fabric together for fitting or to stop them slipping as seams are stitched. The UK term is tacking.

bias strip or binding – a strip of fabric cut on a 45° diagonal to the straight of grain of a piece of fabric. It is used to bind edges, particularly curved edges. It stretches very easily and should be handled with care.

blackout lining – a lining of closely woven fabric, or a plastic-coated fabric, that will block the passage of light. Also known as a light-resistant lining.

blend – a fabric that is a mixture of two materials, such as polyester/cotton, or mohair/wool. The mix can be 50/50 or may be unequal amounts, such as 50 percent merino wool/33 percent microfiber/12 percent cashmere. The exact composition of fabric is usually given on the end of the bolt.

bolt – an amount of fabric, wound onto a round tube or a flattened oval cardboard form. The fabric is usually folded lengthways, right sides together and the amount in a bolt depends on the type of fabric and the manufacturer. Wholesale fabric stores often sell fabric by the bolt, rather than by cut length, so you purchase a larger amount but at a cheaper price per yard/meter.

box valance – a three-dimensional valance that has sides and a front and protrudes from the wall above a drape, covering the drapery heading. *See also* valance, pelmet.

buckram – a stiffened fabric, used to stiffen pelmets and drape headings.

bullion fringe – a thick, heavy and long fringe.

butting – bringing two edges together so that they touch but do not overlap.

canopy – fabric draped or hung over a frame attached to a four-poster bed, or a decorative treatment above a headboard. *See also* corona, half tester.

catch – to attach one piece of fabric to another, generally with a few tiny backstitches made by hand. For instance, a facing could be attached to a seam allowance.

clip – to cut a short distance into a seam allowance or selvage with the point of the scissors. It is used on curved seams, square corners and in similar places, to remove excess fabric so seams will lie flat when pressed.

colorway – any of a range of combinations of colors in which a style or design is available.

composition – the percentage of each material that a fabric is made from. This is generally given on the end of the bolt, but may also be printed or woven in the selvage. It is important to know the composition so you will know how to treat the finished item when it needs cleaning or pressing.

corona – a decorative half-circular frame above the head of a bed, that often supports a canopy. *See also* canopy, half tester.

count – the number of warp and weft fabric threads in an inch of fabric. It is used to indicate the fineness or coarseness of a fabric.

covered lathe – a decorative strip hiding a drapery track when the drapes are open.

cut length – the cut length is a piece of fabric that has been measured and cut. In drapes, it is the length to cut for each width, allowing for the matching of repeats.

directional designs – *see* one-way designs.

drape – the property of a fabric to fall into folds. If it falls gracefully it is said to drape well or have good drape.

dress drapes – drapes that are for show and are not intended—or are not able—to be closed across the window.

dressed drapes – drapes that have had their folds adjusted into even lines and then loosely tied and left to "set", so that when the ties are removed the folds will remain in place. Formal drapes should always be dressed—and dress drapes are usually dressed.

drop/finished drop – the measurement from the top to the bottom of completely finished drapery, with all seams and hems stitched in place.

Glossary

eyelet – small round hole in fabric, which may be hand-stitched or created with a punch and lined with a metal ring that grips the fabric on the reverse. Hand-stitched eyelets are edged with overcast stitching or blanket stitch to stop the edges fraying. Eyelets are used for drapery headings, for decorative effect and to take lacing.

facing – a shaped piece of fabric stitched on the seam line and turned inside to create a finished edge.

finial – turned shape used to end a pole decoratively.

flush window – a window that is set level with the front face of a wall.

four-poster – type of bed with a flat "ceiling" of fabric—or sometimes wood—that covers the entire bed area and is supported by full-height posts that extend upwards from each corner of the bed. Sometimes it also has drapes that can be draw right around to enclose the bed. Also called a tester. See also half tester, canopy, corona.

fullness – an amount of extra fabric allowed across the width of drapes, so they will still have gathers or pleats even when pulled closed across the window.

gathering – a method of controlling fullness by running a double line of large stitches through a fabric, fastening the threads at one end and pulling on the other end to reduce the fabric to a smaller length.

gimp – narrow flat braid or rounded cord of fabric used for trim or as the base of other trims.

grain – this is the direction of the threads making up a woven fabric, so each piece has two—lengthways (warp) and widthways or crosswise (weft).

half-drop repeat – with a half-drop repeat, the motifs repeat across the fabric, but on alternate lines they are offset so each motif falls in the center between the motifs above and below. See also pattern repeat.

half tester – A half tester has a "ceiling" that extends only partway down the bed, cantilevered from above the head end, so the bed does not have full-height foot posts. See also tester, canopy, corona.

heading – the top of drapes or a valance.

hold-back – a solid hoop or decorative knob that is fixed to the wall on each side of drapery. When open, the drapes are hooked back behind the hold-back to hold them in place. See also tie-back.

interlining – a non-woven brushed fabric placed between the lining and the main fabric of drapery to add body, insulation and to help the fabric fold properly.

Italian stringing – a method of opening drapes in which the drapess are fixed at the top, but cording running diagonally across the drape pulls it up from near the bottom into a deep curve towards the top.

leading edge – the edge of drapery that travels across the window.

lambrequins – a flat ornamental drapery across the top and down the side of a window or door, or suspended from the edge of a shelf.

lengthways fold – a fold down the length of a piece of fabric. Very wide fabric on a bolt is generally folded lengthways, with right sides together.

light-resistant lining – see blackout lining.

miter – a diagonal join between two strips of fabric meeting at a square corner.

nap – fabric with nap usually has a short pile and will look different shades from different angles because it catches the light differently. Velvet and velour are both fabrics with nap. When making drapes with a napped fabric, make sure that the pile runs the same way on each width.

neaten – to finish off by pulling loose threads to the wrong side and tying or stitching them in before cutting off. Seam edges can be neatened and prevented from fraying by binding, pinking or zigzag stitching.

one-way designs – designs based on repeating motifs with a distinct top and bottom, so they run in only one direction and will look very different if the fabric is turned upside down. Also called directional designs. When making drapes with a one-way fabric, make sure that the design is running the same way on each width.

overlap – the amount the leading edge of one curtain overlaps the leading edge of other curtain.

panel – flat fabric which is lined only, with weights in the hem to make it hang straight. The panel is then hung from tracking, which is generally attached to the ceiling.

pattern repeat – most patterns are made up of one or more components that repeat along the length and/or width. The length of a pattern repeat is determined by measuring from a set point on a motif to the matching point on the next. In a full drop repeat the rows are all repeated with the motifs directly in line both down and across. See also half-drop repeat.

pelmet – a solid covering that hides the top of window drapery. It may be carved, fretwork, molded or covered in fabric.

pin tuck – a very narrow stitched tuck in fabric. Several are often made in close parallel rows to give a decorative look. *See also* tuck.

pleat – even folds in fabric to add fullness.

portière – a one-sided drape that acts as a door in a corridor, or a window/door covering with rod pockets at top and bottom holding rods that are attached to the wall at one end only, so the panel can swing open.

raw edge – a cut edge of fabric that has not been finished in any way.

recessed window – a window that is set back into an alcove in the wall.

repeat – see pattern repeat.

return – part of the drapery that returns to the wall at the end of the rail—also applies to the outer edge of a pelmet or valance.

right side – in printed fabrics the pattern will be clearer and brighter on the right side, but the difference is not always so obvious. The term is usually abbreviated to RS.

ruffle – a gathered or pleated border also known as a frill.

saddle stitching – a decorative form of stitching done with two needles, where each stitch butts right up to the following one.

seam allowance – the amount of fabric allowed for seams when joining two pieces of fabric together. Usually there is a seam allowance of ⅝ in (1.5 cm), between the cutting line and the seamline.

selvage – this is the finished edge along either side of the length of fabric. These edges will not fray, but it is usually better to avoid incorporating them into drapery as they sometimes pucker up when the fabric is laundered.

slub – an uneven thread or yarn with thicker sections, which may be accidental or by design. When woven the fabric will have random nubs running with the weave. With some fabrics, such as slubbed silk, this is an essential part of the character of the fabric.

stack back – the width of the hung drapes when they are pulled completely open.

straight of grain – threads running lengthways, or parallel to the selvages, are on the straight of grain. Threads running widthways, or from selvage to selvage, are on the cross grain.

swags – a graceful fold of fabric across the top of a window. Often combined with tails.

swatch – small piece of fabric, used as a color sample.

tails – ends of fabric that hang down in decorative folds at each side of a window. Often combined with a swag.

tie-back – a short decorative length of fabric, cording or rope that is either hooked or fixed to the wall and is used to tie back drapes when in the open position.

touch and close tape – a type of fastening that comes in two parts; one half has tiny loops and the other tiny hooks so when pressed together they cling to each other. It is often used for items that need to be unfastened quickly. Also known as hook and loop tape; in the UK it is known as Velcro®.

tuck – stitched fold of fabric, often used as a decorative feature. See also pin tuck.

valance – a soft draped or gathered fabric covering to the top of drapes.

width – the measurement across a piece of fabric. Drapes may be made up of several widths to enable them to cover a window with some fullness.

wrong side – the side of a fabric that will not be seen. In printed fabrics the pattern will be fainter and duller on the wrong side, but the difference is not always so obvious. The term is usually abbreviated to WS.

Index

About the Author

If you don't know my name or have not seen any of my previous books, then let me tell you a little bit about myself, and my work. I was born in London rather a long time ago. My father was in the Navy during the war and afterwards went to work on the English newspaper the *Evening Standard*. My mother was the daughter of a Court Dressmaker, which is perhaps why I went into the "rag trade" at the start of my working life. She was my guide, my tower of strength and she filled me with determination...I miss her to bits!

I left school at 15 and went to business college for a year, against my wishes—my mother was determined I should be a secretary. I ran away from home at 16 and bought a one way ticket to the furthest point £25 would take me: Rome. I worked as a model in Europe for several years, but eventually I came home to London.

It was the height of the sixties and I opened a boutique in Kensington under the name of Harriet—and that is what everyone called me for 18 years. I was clubbing by night and working by day—life was such fun. Harriet soon expanded and we moved from Kensington High Street to the real "rag trade" area, Margaret Street. Soon Harriet was in all the major department stores in London and New York. Life was busy—but tiring, and by this time I was married and had my wonderful daughter and I wanted to spend time with her. So I went on holiday for 10 days. I came back bored out of my mind and realised I needed to work!

I was looking for a new challenge when my best friend, Jean, asked if I would pay for her to train as a beauty therapist. When she qualified she asked if I would like to go into business with her. I wasn't really interested in beauty therapies, but liked the idea of running a beauty salon so we opened Secrets a few months later. The combination of my business brain and Jean's natural flair meant we were an instant success, but I found that I hated the beauty business, so I decided to move on.

Being an interior designer seemed to be all the rage in the eighties, and I decided to give that a go. So there I was, with a big pile of carpet samples and lots of fabrics. I put an advert in *House and Garden* and sat by the telephone until one day I got my first client. Whatever I didn't know I made up as I went along and I never looked back. After a few years I had a big client list, including many well-known faces and many multi-national companies.

My first sketchbook of drape designs was just a few rough sketches put together with a paperclip—it was useful for me to have in my bag to show clients a few of my ideas. It was always a problem trying to explain how a covered lathe worked, or which way the drapes would pull in a bay window. The sketchbook saved me having to draw things afresh for each individual client.

Soon other designers heard about my sketchbook and they began to ask for a copy. Six months later my husband set up a desk in the garage where he collated the pages before taking them to be laminated. The first Sketchbooks were collections of single laminated pages and cost £35 each... we sold thousands of them!

For some years I lived in France, but now I am home in England and glad to be. I live with my companion Dawson and I have a wonderful daughter who is an amazing photographer and who fills me with joy. I always try to keep all my books up to date, and I make sure that if there is a new trend in U.S. or Europe it is shown in my books as soon as possible. The Sketchbooks keep selling and I keep working as a designer and writer... but I have a few new ideas up my sleeve, so watch this space!

I would like to thank Chrissie Carriere for her wonderful illustrations, Holly Jolliffe for the photography, Malena Burgess for the styling and all the fabric companies and suppliers listed below.

Picture credits: pp. 2, 6, 72, 108 and 148 courtesy of Designers Guild (www.designersguild.com); pp. 26, 46, 64, 176 and 248 courtesy of Osborne and Little (www.osborneandlittle.com); p. 70 courtesy of Byron & Byron (www.byronandbyron.com); p.210 courtesy of And So To Bed (www.andsotobed.co.uk). All other photography by Holly Jolliffe.

Fabric swatches: p.18 L–R Alton-Brooke, Colefax & Fowler, Jane Churchill, Parkertex, Colefax & Fowler, Zimmer & Rohde, Colefax & Fowler, Mulberry; p.19 L–R Osborne & Little, Romo, Designers Guild, Manuel Canovas, Colefax & Fowler, Alton-Brooke, Designers Guild, Designers Guild, Alton-Brooke; p.20 L–R Colefax & Fowler, Nina Campbell/Osborne & Little, Romo, Osborne & Little, Malabar, GP&J Baker, Romo, Malabar; p.21 L–R Manuel Canovas, Manuel Canovas, Jane Churchill, Lorca, Designers Guild, Colefax & Fowler, Sheila Coombes, Sheila Coombes; p.22 L–R Designers Guild, Lorca, Manuel Canovas, J. Robert Scott, Jane Churchill, Lorca, Jane Churchill, Designers Guild, Zimmer & Rohde; p.23 L–R Kravet, Osborne & Little, Designers Guild, Designers Guild, Zimmer & Rohde, Designers Guild, Kravet.

Wendy Baker
London 2008